Spiritual Revival

Spiritual Revival

Glenn L. Pace

Deseret Book Company
Salt Lake City, Utah

Library of Congress Cataloging-in-Publication Data

Pace, Glenn L.
    Spiritual revival / Glenn L. Pace.
      p. cm.
    Includes bibliographical references and index.
    ISBN 0-87579-733-4
    1. Spiritual life—Mormon authors. 2. Church of Jesus Christ of Latter-day Saints—Membership. 3. Mormon Church—Membership.
I. Title.
BX8656.P29 1993
248.4'8332—dc20   93-9902
                                          CIP

Printed in the United States of America

10   9   8   7   6   5   4   3   2   1

Contents

Preface

In 1991 I published a book entitled *Spiritual Plateaus*. The warm response to that effort has been a source of encouragement to communicate once again with the members of the Church. *Spiritual Plateaus* was a vehicle intended to help a person progress spiritually.

This new book, *Spiritual Revival*, is intended to be a jump start to that vehicle. Perhaps I should have called it *Spiritual Plateaus: The Beginning*, for if I had had both of these subjects in mind when I began writing my first book, I probably would have written this one first.

On October 3, 1992, I gave a ten-minute talk in general conference that I called "Spiritual Revival." Since I was one of the first speakers, I was able to enjoy the rest of the conference and listen carefully to the other messages. One of the predominate themes in this conference was what we should be doing to fine-tune our lives in order to cope with the time in which we live. Hearing what others said intensified my own feelings and gave me a desire to spend more than ten minutes with members of the Church on this subject. This book is the result of that desire. My conference talk serves to introduce my theme, spiritual revival.

Spiritual Revival

When I was young I was overly dependent on my older sister. For example, I was a fussy eater, and when we went to visit our grandparents I was constantly faced with being offered food I didn't like. To minimize my embarrassment, when the plate was passed to me, I would turn to my sister and ask, "Collene, do I like this?"

If the food was familiar and she knew I didn't like it, she would say, "No, he doesn't like that."

I could then say to Grandma, "She's right, I don't like it."

If the food was something we hadn't eaten before she would say, "Just a minute," and taste it, and then tell me if I liked it or not. If she said I didn't like it, no amount of coaxing could get me to eat it.

I know it is past time for me to rely on my own taste buds and stop denying myself healthy food just because my sister once told me I didn't like it.

On a much more serious note, I believe the time has come for all of us to feast on the fruit of our own testimony as opposed to the testimony of another person. The testimony of which I speak is much deeper than knowing the Church is true. We need to progress to the point of knowing we are true to the Church. We also need to increase our capacity to receive personal revelation. It is one thing to receive a witness that Joseph Smith saw God and Christ. It is quite another to have spiritual self-confidence in our ability to receive the revelation to which we are entitled.

Many of us take the blessings of the gospel for granted. It is as if we are passengers on the train of the Church, which has been moving forward gradually and methodically. Sometimes we have looked out the window and thought, *That looks kind of fun out there. This train is so restrictive.* So we have jumped off and gone and played in the woods for a while. Sooner or later, we find it isn't as much fun as Lucifer makes it appear or we get critically injured, so we work our way back to the tracks and see the train ahead. With a determined sprint we catch up to it, breathlessly wipe the perspiration from our foreheads, and thank the Lord for repentance.

While on the train, we can see the world and some of our own members outside laughing and having a great time. They taunt us and coax us to get off. Some throw logs and rocks on the tracks to try and derail it. Others run alongside the tracks, and while they may never go play in the woods, they just can't seem to get on the train. Still others try to run ahead and too often take the wrong turn.

I would propose that the luxury of getting on and off the train as we please is fading. The speed of the train is increasing. The woods are getting much too dangerous, and the fog and darkness are moving in.

Although our detractors might as well "stretch forth [their] puny arm[s] to stop the Missouri river in its decreed course, or to turn it up stream" (D&C 121:33) as to derail this train, they are occasionally successful in coaxing individuals off. With all the prophecies we have seen fulfilled, what great event are we awaiting prior to saying, "Count me in"? What more do we need to see or experience before we get on the train and stay on it until we reach our destination? It is time for a spiritual revival. It is time to dig down deep within ourselves and rekindle our own light.

President Joseph F. Smith said: "One fault to be avoided by the Saints, young and old, is the tendency to live on borrowed light, . . . [and] to permit . . . the light within them to be reflected, rather than original." (*Gospel Doctrine* [Salt Lake City: Deseret Book, 1939], p. 87.)

The whole world seems to be in commotion. Today's news is filled with accounts of large-scale famine, civil unrest, and natural disasters. Even more devastating in the long run is the spiritually destructive hurricane of disobedience to God's commandments that is engulfing the world. This horrible storm is blowing the moral fiber out of the nations of the earth and leaving the land in moral desolation. Many people seem to be oblivious to this hurricane and have become so desensitized that they don't even feel a breeze.

We are following a cycle that was repeated over and over again in the Book of Mormon. As the Lord tells us, "In the day of their peace they esteemed lightly my counsel;

but, in the day of their trouble, of necessity they feel after me." (D&C 101:8.)

We shouldn't be too surprised, therefore, that the Lord is allowing some wake-up calls to jar us loose from apathy, just as he has done in previous dispensations. In the book of Helaman, Nephi said, "And thus we see that except the Lord doth chasten his people with many afflictions, . . . they will not remember him." (Helaman 12:3.)

In our dispensation, the Lord has said, "My people must needs be chastened until they learn obedience, if it must needs be, by the things which they suffer." (D&C 105:6.)

To some, the events unfolding in the world today are frightening. This is not a time to panic, but it is definitely a time to prepare. What can we do to better prepare ourselves for that which is at our doorstep? It is simple. We need to get back to basics and learn obedience. When we are obedient, we follow the first principles of the gospel and place our faith in our Lord and Savior, repent of our sins, and are baptized and receive the Holy Ghost to guide us. We read and ponder the scriptures, pray for direction in our lives, and look for ways to help others who are going through difficult times. We share the gospel with people living on earth and make it possible for saving ordinances to be performed for those who have passed beyond the veil.

During this conference and on many other occasions we will be taught by the Lord's anointed servants. These prophets, seers, and revelators receive revelation relative to the kingdom, revelation to which their mantle entitles them. We follow the Brethren. Finally, we prepare ourselves to receive an endowment in the temple. If we remain faithful, this endowment literally gives us additional power to overcome the sins of the world and "stand in holy places." (D&C 45:32.)

I make a special appeal to the youth. You will remain much safer and be infinitely happier if you will place your energy into current obedience rather than saving it for future repentance. When we are obedient, we establish a base from which the challenges of the future can be addressed.

In spite of our obedience, trials and tribulations will come our way. Disasters and tribulation are not always for the punishment of the wicked; often they are for the sanctification of the righteous. We admire the early members of the Church for their faithfulness through their numerous trials. It is interesting to contemplate whether they succeeded in facing their obstacles because of their spirituality or whether they were spiritual because of the obstacles they faced.

Into each of our lives come golden moments of adversity. This painful friend, adversity, breaks our hearts, drops us to our knees, and makes us realize we are nothing without our Lord and Savior. It makes us plead all the night long, and into the next day and sometimes for weeks and months, for reassurance. But ultimately, just as surely as the day follows the night, as we remain true and faithful, adversity leads us straight into the outstretched arms of the Savior.

I have tried to understand why we must experience tribulation before we can experience the ultimate communication. It seems there is an intense concentration that must be obtained before our pleadings reach our Father in heaven and, perhaps even more importantly, before he can get through to us. Sometimes we must be straining very hard to hear the still small voice. Before we can be taught things hidden from the world, we must be on a spiritual frequency that is out of this world. Adversity can help fine-tune this frequency. Even the Savior communicated more intensely with our Father in heaven when he was in agony. When the Lord was in Gethsemane, Luke recorded, "being in an agony he prayed more earnestly." (Luke 22:44.)

The challenge for each of us, in order to prevent having to receive constant wake-up calls, is to remain obedient once we have turned upward. As the storm clears, it is possible to stay in tune by being valiant in our testimonies. We can then enjoy reprieves—sometimes long ones—and have a taste of heaven on earth. Nevertheless, it does not seem to be in the plan to have a whole lifetime of bliss if our goal is increased spirituality and perfection.

It is my hope that each of us will experience a spiritual revival as we become more obedient. This increased depth of spirituality will help give us the perspective we need to face today's adversities and the strength we need for tomorrow.

While the world is in commotion, the kingdom is intact. We are living in the greatest and most exciting part of our dispensation since the Restoration itself. We plead with everyone to become active participants in building the kingdom. This is the hour of our opportunity, to which I testify.

1

Challenges of the Last Days

The Lord has said, "The voice of warning shall be unto all people, by the mouths of my disciples, whom I have chosen in these last days." (D&C 1:4.) Volumes have been written on prophecies of the last days. It is not my objective to write another. However, I would like to point out that we are well into the fulfillment of many of these prophecies, and, therefore, we should be feeling a sense of urgency. Whenever this issue is discussed, there are some who panic and develop an "Armageddon" mentality. A few even suggest that the Brethren are not current on the gravity of our situation. I don't want to sensationalize the issue, but the words of both the scriptures and modern-day prophecies are relevant. These things must all be placed in proper perspective, which includes listening carefully to the current prophets, seers, and revelators as opposed to following our next-door neighbor into the wilderness.

God has given us laws, and any violation of those laws has natural consequences. We all know this will be true on judgment day, for he has said:

> They who are not sanctified through the law which I have given unto you, even the law of Christ, must inherit another kingdom, even that of a terrestrial kingdom, or that of a telestial kingdom. For he who is not able to abide the law of a celestial kingdom cannot abide a celestial glory. And he who cannot abide the law of a terrestrial kingdom cannot abide a terrestrial glory. And he who cannot abide the law of a telestial kingdom cannot abide a telestial glory; therefore he is not meet for a kingdom of glory. Therefore he must abide a kingdom which is not a kingdom of glory.
>
> And again, verily I say unto you, the earth abideth the law of a celestial kingdom, for it filleth the measure of its creation, and transgresseth not the law — wherefore, it shall be sanctified; yea, notwithstanding it shall die, it shall be quickened again, and shall abide the power by which it is quickened, and the righteous shall inherit it. . . .
>
> All kingdoms have a law given; and there are many kingdoms; for there is no space in the which there is no kingdom; and there is no kingdom in which there is no space, either a greater or a lesser kingdom. And unto every kingdom is given a law; and unto every law there are certain bounds also and conditions.
>
> All beings who abide not in those conditions are not justified. (D&C 88:21–26, 36–39.)

We know that at judgment day, the demands of justice for breaking laws will be satisfied. To a large degree this is true also while we still live on the earth. Though there is often no immediate "punishment" for transgression of God's laws, consequences usually begin to be recognizable over a period of time. This is becoming very apparent in our day when heinous sins are being committed. Indeed, we seem to be on the brink of the earth's cup of iniquity overflowing.

The Lord has also warned and continues to warn his children concerning the need to repent in order that they may escape the natural consequences of transgression. "And it shall come to pass, because of the wickedness of the world, that I will take vengeance upon the wicked, for they will not repent; for the cup of mine indignation is full; for behold, my blood shall not cleanse them if they hear me not." (D&C 29:17.)

These times are near. In 1830, the Lord said, "The hour is nigh and the day soon at hand when the earth is ripe." (D&C 29:9.) I once asked President Marion G. Romney how much time he thought we had. He answered by reading this scripture and then said, "I don't know when that time will come. All I know is that it is 150 years nigher than when the revelation was received."

Since 1830, modern-day prophets have warned the inhabitants of the earth about the consequences of continuing in sin. We are witnesses to the fact that in spite of those warnings, the world is getting more wicked. The Lord has told us some of the consequences of ignoring these warnings:

"After your testimony cometh the testimony of earthquakes, . . . and . . . the testimony of the voice of thunderings, and the voice of lightnings, and the voice of tempests, and the voice of the waves of the sea heaving themselves beyond their bounds. And all things shall be in commotion; and surely, men's hearts shall fail them; for fear shall come upon all people." (D&C 88:89–91.)

"In that day shall be heard of wars and rumors of wars, and the whole earth shall be in commotion, . . . and [men] shall say that Christ delayeth his coming until the end of the earth. And the love of men shall wax cold, and iniquity shall abound." (D&C 45:26–27.)

"There shall be men standing in that generation, that shall not pass until they shall see an overflowing scourge; for a desolating sickness shall cover the land. But my disciples shall stand in holy places, and shall not be moved; but among the wicked, men shall lift up their voices and curse God and die. And there shall be earthquakes also in divers places, and many desolations; yet men will harden their hearts against me, and they will take up the sword, one against another, and they will kill one another." (D&C 45:31–33.)

"I, the Lord, am angry with the wicked; I am holding my Spirit from the inhabitants of the earth. . . . And the saints also shall hardly escape; nevertheless, I, the Lord, am with them, and will come down in heaven from the presence of my Father and consume the wicked with unquenchable fire." (D&C 63:32, 34.)

"For I, the Almighty, have laid my hands upon the nations, to scourge them for their wickedness. And plagues shall go forth, and they shall not be taken from the earth until I have completed my work, which shall be cut short in righteousness." (D&C 84:96–97.)

I have spared the reader the discomfort of reading some of the prophecies of an even more distasteful nature. Most of those will be fulfilled as we get closer to the Millennium. My intent has been to concentrate on events that are upon us now. Supporting my assumption that the Lord's warnings have begun are warnings from modern-day prophets.

President Wilford Woodruff asked, "What is the matter with the world today? What has created this change that we see coming over the world? What is the meaning of all these mighty events that are taking place? The meaning is, these angels that have been held for many years in the temple of our God have got their liberty to go out and commence their mission and their work in the earth, and they are here today in the earth." (*Millennial Star* 56 [October 8, 1894]: 643.)

President Joseph Fielding Smith once said, "I went over the newspapers and over the magazines and jotted down year by year the destructions, the commotions among men, everything in the nature of a calamity, and to my great astonishment each year they increased, and they have been increasing ever since I quit making that record." He referred to a study in which a group of scholars concluded that "war has tended to increase over all Europe in late centuries. . . . All commendable hopes that war will disappear in the near future are based on nothing more substantial than hope of a belief in miracles." President Smith then concluded, "If prophecy is to be fulfilled, there awaits the world a conflict more dreadful than any the world has yet seen." (*Signs of the Times* [Salt Lake City: Deseret Book, 1952], pp. 116, 120.)

Elder Bruce R. McConkie elaborated on this issue in detail at a welfare session of general conference in 1979:

> I stand before the Church this day and raise a warning voice. It is a prophetic voice, for I shall say only what the apostles and prophets have spoken concerning our day. . . . For the moment we live in a day of peace and

prosperity but it shall not ever be thus. Great trials lie ahead. All of the sorrows and perils of the past are but a foretaste of what is yet to be. And we must prepare ourselves temporally and spiritually. . . .

Be it remembered that tribulations lie ahead. There will be wars in one nation and kingdom after another until war is poured out upon all nations and two hundred million men of war mass their armaments at Armageddon. Peace has been taken from the earth, the angels of destruction have begun their work, and their swords shall not be sheathed until the Prince of Peace comes to destroy the wicked and usher in the great Millennium.

There will be earthquakes and floods and famines. The waves of the sea shall heave themselves beyond their bounds, the clouds shall withhold their rain, and the crops of the earth shall wither and die. There will be plagues and pestilence and disease and death. An overflowing scourge shall cover the earth and a desolating sickness shall sweep the land. Flies shall take hold of the inhabitants of the earth, and maggots shall come in upon them. (See D&C 29:14-20.) "Their flesh shall fall from off their bones, and their eyes from their sockets." (D&C 29:19.) Bands of Gadianton robbers will infest every nation, immorality and murder and crime will increase, and it will seem as though every man's hand is against his brother. . . .

It is one of the sad heresies of our time that peace will be gained by weary diplomats as they prepare treaties of compromise, or that the Millennium will be ushered in because men will learn to live in peace and to keep the commandments, or that the predicted plagues and promised desolations of latter days can in some way be avoided. We must do all we can to proclaim peace, to avoid war, to heal disease, to prepare for natural disasters—but with it all, that which is to be shall be. . . .

We do not know when the calamities and troubles of the last days will fall upon any of us as individuals or upon bodies of the Saints. The Lord deliberately withholds from us the day and hour of his coming and of the tribulations which shall precede it—all as part of the testing and probationary experiences of mortality. He simply tells us to watch and be ready. (*Ensign*, May 1979, pp. 92–93.)

In the October 1992 general conference, Elder M. Russell Ballard spoke of the apparent increase in tribulations during the last few years:

These are difficult times, when the forces of nature seem to be unleashing a flood of "famines, and pestilences, and earthquakes, in divers places." [See Matthew 24:7.]

Recently, I read a newspaper article that cited statistics from the U.S. Geological Survey indicating that earthquakes around the world are increasing in frequency and intensity. According to the article, only two major earthquakes, earthquakes measuring at least six on the Richter scale, occurred during the 1920s. In the 1930s the number increased to five, and then decreased to four during the 1940s. But in the 1950s, nine major earthquakes occurred, followed by fifteen during the 1960s, forty-six during the 1970s, and fifty-two during the 1980s. Already almost as many major earthquakes have occurred during the 1990s as during the entire decade of the 1980s.

The world is experiencing violent disorders, both physical as well as social. Here in the United States, we are still reeling from two incredibly destructive hurricanes. People in the Philippines see no end to the devastation of the volcanic eruption of Mt. Pinatubo. Famine grips portions of Africa, where tragic human suffering is prevalent. To a lesser degree, hunger afflicts millions, even in countries that have a high standard of living.

Political unrest, warfare, and economic chaos prevail

in many parts of the world, and the plagues of pornography, drug misuse, immorality, AIDS, and child abuse become more oppressive with each passing day. The media busily satisfies an apparently insatiable appetite of audiences to witness murder, violence, nudity, sex, and profanity. Is not this the day of which Moroni spoke when he recorded: "Behold, I speak unto you as if ye were present, and yet ye are not. But behold, Jesus Christ hath shown you unto me, and I know your doing." (Morm. 8:35.) And then he prophesied of conditions of the world as they are today. (*Ensign,* November 1992, p. 31.)

Some of the destruction going on is spiritual, and those without ears to hear and eyes to see are completely unaware. President George Q. Cannon recognized this truth a century ago: "It is true, He is not coming out in every case in His anger to destroy us; but the work of destruction is operating silently among us. I do not mean physical destruction altogether but spiritual destruction. It is operating among us, and because of the process being silent, the people do not perceive it. Men and women are dropping off like worm-eaten apples from our trees. They are losing their faith and their standing; and family after family, member after member is disappearing and being forgotten. I call this a work of spiritual destruction, for when men and women lose their faith, they are spiritually destroyed. Their names are blotted out of the records of the just, and their condition is a most awful one." (*Gospel Truth* [Salt Lake City: Deseret Book, 1987], p. 41.)

Natural disasters occur in such a way that the spiritually illiterate fail to recognize their significance. Those who are not in tune give no credence to the prophecies and fail to see any connection between the passing events and the sinful condition of the world. President Cannon explained:

> The Lord works in the midst of this people by natural means, and the greatest events that have been spoken of by the holy Prophets will come along so naturally as the consequence of certain causes that unless our eyes are enlightened by the Spirit of God and the spirit of revelation rests on us, we will fail to see that these are the events predicted by the holy Prophets. . . .
>
> They will come along in so natural a manner, the Lord will bring them to pass in such a way that they will not be accepted by the people, except by those who can comprehend the truth, as the fulfillment of the predictions of the Prophets. It requires the Spirit of God to enable men and women to understand the things of God; it requires the Spirit of God to enable the people to comprehend the work of God and to perceive His movements and providences among the children of men. The man who is destitute of the Spirit of God cannot comprehend the work of God.
>
> A reader of the prophecies of ancient and modern times would naturally imagine that when the stupendous events which they mention should take place the world would be convinced of the work of God and would repent of their sins. But it is a remarkable fact that prophecy may be fulfilled in the plainest and the most unmistakable manner and yet the great bulk of mankind refuse to believe that that which they see is the fulfillment. (*Gospel Truth*, p. 36.)

We need to wake up and realize we are well into the fulfillment of the prophecies. We need to realize how ripe the world is getting in iniquity. There are no sins that were practiced at the time of Noah, Sodom and Gomorrah, or the darkest times in the Book of Mormon that are not running rampant today. Elder Cannon compared the people at his time to those living at the time of Noah: "The inhabitants of the earth did this in the days of Noah. They did not believe there would be any flood. They went on enjoying themselves in their way, notwithstanding the message that Noah delivered to them. But still the flood came, and the hardened nations were drowned, and the earth was cleansed from their presence." (*Gospel Truth*, p. 38.)

In 1942, Joseph Fielding Smith expressed the opinion that the world was as wicked at that time as at the time of Noah.

> I believe that the world today is just as wicked, just as corrupt as it was in the days of Noah. . . . The Lord said that the days preceding his second coming would be like the days of Noah, that is, "all flesh has corrupted its way upon the earth." [Moses 8:29.] Naturally someone will wonder why, when in the days of Noah he and his family were the only ones saved and yet today there are thousands of people who have obeyed the commandments and come into the Church from all parts of the world, that I make a statement such as this. Let me call your attention to a condition which prevailed in the days of Enoch which makes all the difference in the world. In his day the Lord gathered together all the righteous and they with Enoch were taken from the earth, and later before the flood if any repented and accepted the truth they too were caught up to the people of Enoch, so that when the time came to cleanse the earth with water, only Noah and his family remained of the righteous, and they were left that the race of mankind might be perpetuated after the flood. . . .
>
> The flood was nothing more nor less than the cleansing of the earth by baptism. Once again in the near

future the earth will be baptized, not by water, for the Lord covenanted with Enoch that He would not again destroy the world by water, but at the coming of our Lord the earth is to receive a baptism of fire and the Holy Ghost.

If the Lord should do today what He did before the flood, and remove from the earth all the righteous, I am convinced that the condition would be just as bad as it was before, and that among the ungodly the wickedness is just as great as it was in the days of Noah. (*Signs of the Times,* pp. 6–8.)

I don't know how to compare our time to Noah's. I wasn't there. I do know Satan is here today with his kingdom and all of his secret combinations, and that he has blinded the world in general with more subtle lies designed to make the commandments of God appear old-fashioned. I feel the way President Cannon felt regarding how deaf and blind people are to the fulfillment of prophecies that are in plain sight: "Notwithstanding these things have been fulfilled no attention is paid to them. The inhabitants of the earth are deaf and blind to all these evidences of God's displeasure and warning. . . . If we did not have evidence of this blindness on the part of the people, it would be almost impossible to convince anyone that it could exist and that men could be so stupid and obstinate as to resist testimonies of so wonderful a character, especially when they have been foretold with such great plainness." (*Gospel Truth,* p. 37.)

Often when I get into a discussion on the increase of signs of the times, someone will say something like this: "I don't think there is an increase in disasters, but an increase in our capacity to know about them. With modern communications we are just more aware." I was amused to see President Cannon address this question in his own day. In 1890, he said:

"One of the most notable features in the news of the day is the frequency with which catastrophes of various kinds are published. The inhabitants of the earth are suffering from judgments of the most terrible character; but they appear to make no impression upon them. The remark is frequently heard, when allusion is made to these events, 'Oh, these disasters always have occurred. We hear more of them now because of the telegraph, which collects details from all parts of the earth.' In this way mankind console themselves with the idea that there is nothing in these occurrences to be startled at, and their hearts are hardened against the testimony of the servants of God and the testimony of God's judgments." (*Gospel Truth*, p. 37.)

What Brother Cannon learned in his day by telegraph, we see today on color television sets live via satellite. People in our day within and without the Church rationalize the seriousness of the situation by claiming the problem isn't increased disasters or increased sin, but merely increased reporting of them. I grow weary of people saying that such things as immorality and child abuse aren't really any worse, but just more public.

As I have quoted past and current prophets, I know that some listeners have thought, "We've been hearing this for 160 years now." I would remind such skeptics that another group living upon this land made similar rationalizations:

"And it came to pass that in the commencement of the ninety and second year, behold, the prophecies of the prophets began to be fulfilled more fully; for there began to be greater signs and greater miracles wrought among the people. But there were some who began to say that the time was past for the words to be fulfilled, which were spoken by Samuel, the Lamanite. And they began to rejoice over their brethren, saying: Behold the time is past, and the words of Samuel are not fulfilled; therefore, your joy and your faith concerning this thing hath been vain.

"And it came to pass that they did make a great uproar throughout the land; and the people who believed began to be very sorrowful, lest by any means those things which had been spoken might not come to pass." (3 Nephi 1:4–7.)

Within months of these sayings, the Savior was born in Bethlehem.

At the beginning of this chapter, I explained that my purpose was not to treat in any detail the prophecies of the last days. That has been done by others to the point that at times, I believe, it is overdone. Some members of the Church are obsessed with prophecies of the last days. My testimony is that we needn't wait for tomorrow to see the prophecies fulfilled. They are being fulfilled today. My fear is that we are not well enough prepared for what is already on our plate. I personally do not want to be guilty of ignoring the Lord's call and warning. Nothing would be more tragic than to have the last line of the following scripture apply to me:

"How oft have I called upon you by the mouth of my servants, and by the ministering of angels, and by mine own voice, and by the voice of thunderings, and by the voice of lightnings, and by the voice of tempests, and by the voice of earthquakes, and great hailstorms, and by the voice of famines and pestilences of every kind, and by the great sound of a trump, and by the voice of judgment, and by the voice of mercy all the day long, and by the voice of glory and honor and the riches of eternal life, and would have saved you with an everlasting salvation, but ye would not!" (D&C 43:25.)

One of the saddest of all scriptures to me is the Savior's cry over Jerusalem: "O Jerusalem, Jerusalem, thou that killest the prophets, and stonest them which are sent unto thee, how often would I have gathered thy children together, even as a hen gathereth her chickens under her wings, and ye would not!" (Matthew 23:37.)

I don't want to hear "Oh, America, America!" under the same condemnation. My whole purpose in writing this book is to call for a spiritual revival in order that we can mitigate the problems ahead.

In addition to experiencing our own spiritual revival, we need to minister to those who have failed thus far to do so and who are experiencing the natural consequences of a sinful world. We have much to offer. In fact, we have everything to offer the world—indeed, the only thing that can heal the deep wounds of a failing society.

2

Responsibilities in the Last Days

How should we respond in a positive manner to the pain and sorrow we see all around us, much of which is the result of the world refusing to repent? Many have been warned and most have not listened. Do we have a responsibility to the disobedient as well as to the innocent? This reminds me of experiences I have had with my own children.

Perhaps you have had an experience similar to this: You are relaxing at the end of a long day. Suddenly the silence and serenity of the moment are shattered by the piercing scream of one of your children. You bolt out of your chair and meet the child, who is screaming hysterically as he runs up the front steps. It is obvious he has a cut that will require stitches. In a fraction of a second you form an opinion of what has taken place. Consequently, the first words out of your mouth, rather than words of sympathy and comfort, are, "Oh, son, why can't you be more careful? When are you going to learn to mind me? I've told you a thousand times not to play on the garage roof!"

Our children will testify that we never claim to have told them two, three, nine, or fifteen times; we always claim to have told them a thousand times.

Just as earthly parents issue warnings to their children, so the Lord warns *his* children. Through the Prophet Joseph Smith he has told us, "This is a day of warning, and not a day of many words. For I, the Lord, am not to be mocked in the last days." (D&C 63:58.) In the Doctrine and Covenants are many warnings concerning our days and the things that will come to pass.

It may be an understatement to say the Lord's warnings have begun. How are we responding to the cries for help from God's children? Do we ask, "Why don't you be more careful?" "Why don't you mind the Lord?" "Our Church leaders have told you a thousand times to change your behavior."

Before discussing how we should respond, I would like to suggest, in today's vernacular, two "attitude adjustments":

1. *We need to overcome fatalism.*

We know the prophecies of the future. We know the final outcome. We know that the world collectively will not repent, and that, as a consequence, the last days will be filled with much pain and suffering. Therefore, we could throw up our hands and do nothing but pray for the end to come so that the millennial reign could begin. To do so would forfeit our right to participate in the grand event we are all awaiting. We must all become players in the winding-up scene, not spectators. We must do all we can to prevent calamities, and then do everything possible to assist and comfort the victims of tragedies that do occur.

Lehi set an excellent example for us in the way he handled his knowledge relative to the future of Laman and Lemuel. Early in his sons' lives, Lehi had a vision in which he learned that they would not partake of the fruit of the tree of life. Immediately after the vision, however, "he did exhort them . . . with all the feeling of a tender parent, that they would hearken to his words, that perhaps the Lord would be merciful to them." (1 Nephi 8:37.)

During the remainder of his life, Lehi saw confirmations of that vision in his sons' actions time and time again. However, he never gave up but labored with them and loved them. Even near death, with no sign of their ever changing, he said, "And now that my soul might have joy in you, and that my heart might leave this world with gladness because of you, that I might not be brought down with grief and sorrow to the grave, arise from the dust, my sons, and be men." (2 Nephi 1:21.) Lehi never gave up. He labored with his sons to his dying breath.

This same set of scriptures tells us of the world's ultimate destiny. Are we any less obliged, even though we know our numbers will always be few, to give our lives to the spreading of the good news and extending love to all mankind? (See 1 Nephi 14:12.)

The great prophet Mormon set another example worthy of emulation. He lived at a time that was hopeless. Imagine wickedness to the extent described in the scripture: "Wickedness did prevail upon the face of the whole land, insomuch that the Lord did take away his beloved disciples, and the work of miracles and of healing did cease because of the iniquity of the people. And there were no gifts from the Lord, and the Holy Ghost did not come upon any, because of their wickedness and unbelief." (Mormon 1:13–14.)

Despite this hopeless situation, Mormon, at a very young age, led the armies of his people, explaining, "Notwithstanding their wickedness I had led them many times to battle, and had loved them, according to the love of God which was in me, with all my heart; and my soul had been poured out in prayer unto my God all the day long for them. . . . And thrice have I delivered them out of the hands of their enemies, and they have repented not of their sins." (Mormon 3:12–13.)

Mormon then received a revelation from the Lord that his people would be "cut off from the face of the earth" (v. 15), which led him to refuse to lead them further for a time. As he witnessed the carnage and destruction, however, he felt compassion for them and repented of his oath because they depended on him so much. He led them in battle until they had all been hewn down except twenty-four, and still he witnessed no repentance. But even with that disappointment, Mormon cried, "O ye fair ones, how could ye have departed from the ways of the Lord! O ye fair ones, how could ye have rejected that Jesus, who stood with open arms to receive you! Behold, if ye had not done this, ye would not have fallen. But behold, ye are fallen, and I mourn your loss . . . and my sorrows cannot bring your return." (Mormon 6:17–18, 20.)

This prophet had Christlike love for a fallen people. Can we be content with loving less? We must press forward with the pure love of Christ to spread the good news of the gospel. As we do so and fight the war of good against evil, light against darkness, and truth against falsehood, we must not neglect our responsibility of dressing the wounds of those who have fallen in battle. There is no room in the kingdom for fatalism.

2. *We must not allow ourselves to find satisfaction in calamities of the last days.*

If we are not careful, we might be tempted to take some satisfaction in seeing the natural consequences of sin unfold. We might feel some vindication for being ignored by most of the world and persecuted and berated by many. As we see earthquakes, wars, famines, disease, poverty, and heartbreak, we might be tempted to click our tongues and say, "Well, we warned them" or, "We told them a thousand times not to engage in those activities."

As we view the casualties of war, we will find among the wounded our own fellow Latter-day Saints who have not been true to their covenants. We will also find those who have fought against our principles with their own ideologies. As we see the long-term results of the behavior of a permissive society unfolding before our eyes, we might be tempted to think of the resultant pain of those affected as their just due. We might also look at general signs of the times with some joy because we know they are a prelude to the Second Coming. We should take a couple of proverbs to heart: "He that is glad at calamities shall not be unpunished" (Proverbs 17:5) and "Rejoice not when thine enemy falleth, and let not thine heart be glad when he stumbleth" (Proverbs 24:17).

On this subject, Job said, "I should have denied the God that is above. If I rejoiced at the destruction of him that hated me, or lifted myself up when evil found him:

neither have I suffered my mouth to sin by wishing a curse to his soul." (Job 31:28–30.)

King Benjamin addressed the sin of judging a person in need very clearly: "Perhaps thou shalt say: The man has brought upon himself his misery; therefore I will stay my hand, and will not give unto him of my food, nor impart unto him of my substance that he may not suffer, for his punishments are just—But I say unto you, O man, whosoever doeth this the same hath great cause to repent. . . . And if ye judge the man who putteth up his petition to you for your substance that he perish not, and condemn him, how much more just will be your condemnation for withholding your substance." He also makes it clear that he is not just speaking of providing food: "I would that ye should impart of your substance to the poor, every man according to that which he hath, such as feeding the hungry, clothing the naked, visiting the sick and administering to their relief, both spiritually and temporally, according to their wants." (Mosiah 4:17–18, 22, 26.)

We know that many wounds are self-inflicted and could have been avoided simply by obedience to gospel principles. However, to click our tongues and shrug it off as "their problem" is not acceptable to the Lord. He said, "Come unto me, *all* ye that labour and are heavy laden, and I will give you rest." (Matthew 11:28; emphasis added.)

Although he does not condone sin, His arms are always open to the sinner. In modern revelation we have been told, "I, the Lord, will forgive whom I will forgive, but of you it is required to forgive all men." (D&C 64:10.)

Our forgiveness must be manifest by reaching out to help mend wounds even when they are the result of transgression. To react in any other way would be akin to setting up a lung-cancer clinic for nonsmokers only. Whether the pain has come to someone who is completely innocent or is something of his or her own making is irrelevant. When someone has been hit by a truck, we don't withhold our help even if it is obvious that person didn't stay in the pedestrian lane, or wait to find out if the light was red or green.

While some of the world's suffering can be traced to an individual's disobedience or lack of judgment, there is wholesale suffering taking place that is not the result of anyone's own mistakes. Millions of people around the world go to sleep hungry. In their waking hours they are racked with disease and other afflictions. The causes are many, varied, and complex. Also, natural disasters fall on the righteous as well as the wicked.

Now, having discussed some attitude adjustments concerning fatalism and the inappropriateness of expressing joy in calamities, what action should we take? What should we be doing as a church and as individuals in response to the mammoth need in the world?

Our numbers are few. For every person in the world who is a member of the Church, there are approximately a thousand who are not. Our resources are limited, and the needs of the world are vast. We cannot do everything, but we must do everything we can.

The Brethren closely monitor the multitude of crises throughout the world and give assistance to a wide range of areas and peoples. Assistance is given where the need seems to be the greatest without consideration to the political or religious ideologies that exist in each country.

Joseph Smith, in response to the question "What is required to constitute good [Church] membership," said,

"He is to feed the hungry, to clothe the naked, to provide for the widow, to dry up the tear of the orphan, to comfort the afflicted, whether in this church, or in any other, or in no church at all, wherever he finds them." (*Times and Seasons*, March 15, 1842, p. 732.)

More recently President Gordon B. Hinckley said, "Where there is stark hunger, regardless of the cause, I will not let political considerations dull my sense of mercy or thwart my responsibility to the sons and daughters of God, wherever they may be or whatever their circumstances." (*Ensign*, May 1985, p. 54.)

As we read accounts or see graphic pictures of human suffering, we are touched and ask, "What can we do?" We may not be in a position to help on a person-to-person basis when the need is many miles away, but we can pray for peace throughout the world and for the well-being of all its inhabitants. We can also fast and increase our fast offerings when we are able, and thus enable the Church to do more.

As far as person-to-person assistance is concerned, the greatest compassionate service each of us can give may be in our own neighborhoods and communities. Wherever we live in the world there is pain and sorrow all around us. As we continue to teach the gospel ideal, we cannot allow ourselves to be blind to situations that are far less than ideal. Whether the pain has come to someone who is completely innocent or is something of the individual's own making is irrelevant. As we reach out to those in need in our communities, we each, individually, need to take more initiative in deciding how we can best be of service. While opportunities to provide individual, hands-on help in countries other than our own are rare, opportunities in our own communities are plentiful. Many problems are best treated on a community basis.

The fact that a particular activity is not sponsored by the Church does not mean it is not worthy of our support. Good things can be done through the Church organization, through community organizations, and often through no formal organization at all. The Lord said, "Men should be anxiously engaged in a good cause, and do many things of their own free will." (D&C 58:27.) As individuals, we should become knowledgeable of the opportunities around us. I fear that some Saints suffer from action paralysis, waiting for the Church to put its stamp of approval on one organization or another. The Church teaches principles. Each of us must use those principles and the Spirit to decide which organizations we will support.

We must reach out beyond the walls of our own church. In humanitarian work, as in other areas of the gospel, we cannot become the salt of the earth if we stay in one lump in the cultural halls of our beautiful meetinghouses. We need not wait for a formal call or an assignment before we become involved in activities that are best carried out on a community or individual basis.

Some of us have been very blessed and have relatively minor problems. Unless we are careful, we can become insensitive or even oblivious to the major problems in the lives of others. We may be very comfortable with our lives as they are. However, we need to stop and look around us. We need to leave our comfort zones in order to receive the ultimate comfort of living with our Father in heaven and His Son.

Martin Luther King, Jr., said, "The ultimate measure of a man is not where he stands in moments of comfort and convenience, but where he stands at times of challenge and controversy. The true neighbor will risk his position, his prestige, and even his life for the welfare of others. In dangerous valleys and hazardous pathways, he will lift some bruised and beaten brother to a higher and more noble life." (*Strength to Love* [New York: Harper and Row, 1963], pp. 20–21.)

When we get emotionally and spiritually involved in helping a person who is in pain, compassion enters our heart. It hurts, but the process lifts some of the pain from another. We get from the experience a finite look into the Savior's pain as he performed the infinite atonement. Through the power of the Holy Ghost, a sanctification takes place within our souls, and we become more like our Savior. We gain a better understanding of what he meant when he said, "Inasmuch as ye have done it unto one of the least of these my brethren, ye have done it unto me." (Matthew 25:40.)

As the last days unfold, we will see all the prophecies fulfilled. We will see today's problems compounded, and we will see new challenges scarcely imaginable at this time. We must reach out to those who are suffering from these events. We must not become fatalistic or judgmental, even if we warn the people in the world about something a thousand times and they heed us not.

I don't wish to dwell any longer on the negative challenges of the last days. The last-day prophecies also contain good news. Daniel prophesied: "In the days of these kings shall the God of heaven set up a kingdom, which shall never be destroyed: and the kingdom shall not be left to other people, but it shall break in pieces and consume all these kingdoms, and it shall stand for ever. Forasmuch as thou sawest that the stone was cut out of the mountain without hands, and that it brake in pieces the iron, the brass, the clay, the silver, and the gold; the great God hath made known to the king what shall come to pass hereafter: and the dream is certain, and the interpretation thereof sure." (Daniel 2:44–45.)

As Latter-day Saints we need a spiritual revival not just to ensure physical and spiritual survival, but also so we can become active participants in bringing to pass the prophesied growth of the kingdom. This is the stone cut out of the mountain, and it will become the literal kingdom to which the Savior will return and over which he will reign.

"The keys of the kingdom of God are committed unto man on the earth, and from thence shall the gospel roll forth unto the ends of the earth, as the stone which is cut out of the mountain without hands shall roll forth, until it has filled the whole earth." (D&C 65:2.)

3

Opportunities
in the Last Days

We may be inclined to think of a spiritual revival in the last days as that which will be necessary as a defense. Perhaps of greater importance is that a revival will help us take the offense in building the kingdom.

In the priesthood session of general conference in 1991, President Gordon B. Hinckley spoke of the beauty of the unfolding of the kingdom:

> The Church is doing very well. We are far from that state of perfection for which we work, but we are trying — and we are making substantial progress. We are growing consistently and remarkably. . . .
>
> More importantly, there is growing faith and faithfulness among the Latter-day Saints. I am encouraged by what I see. Things are getting consistently better. . . . I have served as a stake or general officer of this Church for more than half a century, and I am confident

that never, during all of that time, has a larger percentage of our people been actively engaged in Church responsibility. I submit that this is one of the great success stories of all time. The credit does not belong to us. It is the Lord's success, for this is His work, and we rejoice with Him in that which has been accomplished. . . .

The charge laid upon the Church is almost beyond comprehension. While yet upon the earth the Lord declared: "And this gospel of the kingdom shall be preached in all the world for a witness unto all nations; and then shall the end come." (Matt. 24:14.) Furthermore, the work of the Church is concerned with the eternal welfare of all generations who have lived upon the earth.

No other organization, in my judgment, faces so great a challenge. That challenge, I am confident, will be met by the growing generation and by generations yet to come. To our youth I say, . . . great is your responsibility, tremendous is your opportunity. I am confident that you will be a part of a beautiful pattern of growth and strengthening vitality that will be marvelous to look upon and awesome to experience.

As the Prophet Joseph once said, no man can stop this work from progressing [see *History of the Church*, 4:540].

Many who are clever and deceitful may try to thwart or destroy it, but none will succeed.

And so, to you, my young brethren tonight, I pass the challenge to keep yourselves clean and worthy and to grow in knowledge and understanding, that your part in the future of this great thing which is the work of the Lord may be well performed and add to the building of the kingdom of God in the earth. (*Ensign*, May 1991, pp. 52, 54.)

The last paragraph is especially relevant to one of my main objectives of this book: to emphasize the positive prophecies of the last days being fulfilled and the importance of each of our individual roles in building the kingdom.

The Spirit is being poured out upon the inhabitants of the earth, as promised by Joel and reiterated by Moroni to Joseph Smith: "And it shall come to pass . . . that I will pour out my spirit upon all flesh; and your sons and your daughters shall prophesy, your old men shall dream dreams, your young men shall see visions: And also upon the servants and upon the handmaids in those days will I pour out my spirit." (Joel 2:28–29. See also Joseph Smith–History 1:41.)

This spirit has led and is continuing to lead the honest in heart to the gospel. As stated in the Doctrine and Covenants: "The Spirit giveth light to every man that cometh into the world; and the Spirit enlighteneth every man through the world, that hearkeneth to the voice of the Spirit. And every one that hearkeneth to the voice of the Spirit cometh unto God, even the Father. And the Father teacheth him of the covenant which he has renewed and confirmed upon you, which is confirmed upon you for your sakes, and not for your sakes only, but for the sake of the whole world." (D&C 84:46–48.)

This truth includes the ever-expanding technological advances that make it possible to reach greater numbers of the honest in heart throughout the world. It is inspiring to go to the Grandin Press historical site in Palmyra, New York, and see the effort and sacrifice it took to print the first five thousand copies of the Book of Mormon. Now we can print millions of copies in the same period of time.

We marvel at how difficult it was for Joseph to communicate with the Saints in Missouri when he was living in Kirtland. Today the Brethren can attend a temple dedication halfway around the world on a Saturday and be home for meetings the next Tuesday.

Family history research is rapidly developing to the point that members can sit in their own homes and have computer access to millions of names.

Latter-day Saints can be reached all over the world via satellite broadcast from Temple Square. Telephones allow priesthood leaders to be in close contact with General Authorities of the Church. Documents can be sent instantaneously, when necessary.

Missionary work is being accelerated through the use of sophisticated technology, with media campaigns and beautiful videos for missionaries and members to show investigators.

We are told that we are just scratching the surface of many of these technologies that will enable the Church to accomplish its mission more effectively. These and countless other technological advances are made available by discoveries of individuals who have had access to the pouring out of the Spirit of the Lord in these last days. Unfortunately, not many realize the source of these breakthroughs. Daniel's prophecy is truly being fulfilled: "In the days of these kings shall the God of heaven set up a kingdom, which shall never be destroyed: and the kingdom shall not be left to other people, but it shall break in pieces and consume all these kingdoms, and it shall stand for ever." (Daniel 2:44.)

Events of the past few years have made it possible to fulfill the prophecy to preach the gospel "unto every nation, and kindred, and tongue, and people." (D&C 133:37.) With conversions have come more family history and more temples. We now see the gospel being preached in Eastern Europe, Africa, and other places where just a few short years ago we never dreamed it might be possible. This dynamic growth is one of the most exciting fulfillments of prophecy.

People outside the Church are beginning to notice and are trying to understand these phenomena. An interview with a sociologist named Rodney Stark appeared recently in many newspapers. I quote from the March 7, 1989, edition of the *Arizona Republic,* which titled the article "Mormonism may grow into 'new world religion' ":

> Championing old-fashioned virtues, Mormons are expanding worldwide, their image of decorum sometimes drawing newcomers faster than they can be accommodated.
>
> This is particularly the case in its new mission fields in black Africa, say officials of the Church of Jesus Christ of Latter-day Saints. There and elsewhere, the exceptional growth rate of the American-founded movement is seen as pointing toward its becoming a major, genuinely international religious body, rivaling older churches.
>
> Sociologist Rodney Stark says it shows all the signs of "the rise of a new world religion," an event of a kind that has happened only rarely in history. On the basis of statistical projections, he says, "the Mormons will soon achieve a worldwide following comparable to that of Islam, Buddhism, Christianity, Hinduism and the other dominant world faiths." . . .
>
> "The rapid growth of Mormons has gone amazingly unremarked by outsiders," sociologist Stark says. He says Mormons "stand on the threshold of becoming the first major faith to appear on Earth since the prophet Mohammed rode out of the desert" in the seventh century to launch the Islamic faith of Muslims.

He estimates on the basis of current growth projections that by 2080 there will be as many as 265 million Mormons around the world.

A similar article, entitled "That Old-Time Religion? U.S. Changing Its Tune," appeared in the Salt Lake *Tribune* May 11, 1991:

> Increasingly, the new worshipers are pushing against America's bedrock religious tradition, especially mainline Protestants. Move over, Methodists and Presbyterians. The Moslems (and Mormons and evangelicals) are here. . . .
>
> Mainline Protestant churches have lost some of their distinctions and zeal to bring in new members. This has happened as the denominations downplayed their differences in uniting for social justice causes beyond their members' needs. . . . [George] Barna . . . says that in this final decade of the 20th century, "the fastest-growing religious bodies in America are not Protestant, Catholic, or Jewish. They are the Church of Jesus Christ of Ladder-day [*sic*] Saints (Mormon), Buddhism, Moslem and various New Age sects." Barna heads Barna Research Group of Glendale, Calif., which has conducted extensive church surveys. . . .
>
> The most recent and complete statistics available for 1989, to be published later this year in the 1991 Yearbook of American and Canadian Churches, find there are about 5.9 million Jews in the United States, up from 5.5 million in 1958, and about 57 million Roman Catholics, up from 40 million.
>
> The Protestants' decline has been dramatic. Five of the most prominent denominations—Episcopal, Evangelical Lutheran Church in America, Presbyterian (U.S.A.), United Church of Christ and United Methodist Church—have seen their total membership drop by 3.3

million, or 13 percent, from 1958 through 1989, a fall from 24.5 million to 21.2 million.

Methodists and Presbyterians lost more than 1 million members each, with only the Lutherans among the five experiencing growth, up 7 percent.

Meanwhile, Mormons and Moslems, once merely listed as unquantified components among "other religions" in the United States, now number in the millions.

Researchers disagree about the size of the Mormon Church and the Islamic faith in the United States. But there is consensus that their numbers now warrant tracking them as specific religions.

A graph was included with this article showing the growth of the various churches from 1958 to 1989. Half of the churches show a loss in membership. Leading all denominations in growth was the Mormon church with an increase of approximately 250 percent. Also, every time I read this article, I get a little chuckle. There are two things about it that amuse me. First, the way they spell "the Church of Jesus Christ of Ladder-day Saints." Second, that researchers disagree about the size of the Church. Why didn't they just call us? We know. Amusement aside, the article reminds me of how wonderful it is to live in this part of this dispensation.

To give some perspective on the amazing growth of the Church I have done some rough calculations on the average yearly growth of the Church during the presidency of each of our prophets. The chart on the following page summarizes my findings.

The growth of the Church has many people scratching their heads as they try to understand why our church is growing when other major religions are losing membership. I went through a frustrating experience trying to help

Prophet	Years as President[1]	Church Membership at Death	Average Yearly Growth
Joseph Smith	14	26,000	2,000
Brigham Young	33	115,000	3,000
John Taylor	10	173,000	6,000
Wilford Woodruff	11	267,000	9,000
Lorenzo Snow	3	293,000	9,000
Joseph F. Smith	17	496,000	12,000
Heber J. Grant	27	979,000	18,000
George Albert Smith	6	1,147,000	28,000
David O. McKay	19	2,931,000	94,000
Joseph Fielding Smith	2	3,219,000	144,000
Harold B. Lee	1	3,300,000	81,000
Spencer W. Kimball	12	5,900,000	217,000
Ezra Taft Benson[2]	7	8,400,000	357,000

Source: Deseret News 1991–1992 Church Almanac.

[1] The years as president have been computed from the year one president died to the year his successor died, rather than from the date each president was sustained.

[2] Ezra Taft Benson was still serving at year-end 1992. Years as president and Church membership were computed as of December 31, 1992.

---

a reporter understand why. A national columnist on religion, he came to Salt Lake City to interview various leaders of the Church. He was sent to my office to discuss welfare, but he couldn't get off the subject of "Why and how?" He had just been in a meeting with a member of the Quorum of the Twelve and apparently didn't want to believe the real reason for the growth. It isn't complicated to anyone with a testimony. The Church is true. When the Lord's sheep hear the message, they feel the testimony of the Holy Ghost and they join the Church.

The reporter, however, wanted to discuss intellectual

reasons. He finally settled in on one big question. How do you get 45,000 young men, young women, and couples to serve missions? "Especially young, nineteen-year-old men," he emphasized.

I went around and around with what is taught at family home evenings, Primary, priesthood meetings, and so forth, and how young people learn from early childhood about the importance of serving a mission, and by the time they reach young adulthood, they are ready to accept a call. After listening patiently, he shook his head and said, "No, I'm not buying."

Having come full circle, I went back to the real reason. "Assume for just a moment," I said, "that you believe that God the Father and His Son Jesus Christ appeared to Joseph Smith and informed him that he would be the vehicle through whom the gospel would be restored to the earth in its fulness. You also believe the current president of the Church is a prophet. From the pulpit at general conference you hear him say that every worthy young man in the Church should plan to serve a mission and every young man should be worthy. You then receive a letter with his signature on it, calling you on a mission. Would you go?"

To my dismay, he answered, "I've read the history of your church and I've talked to your critics and my leanings are that what you just told me is a fabrication."

I thought, *Oh, my goodness, this man is dense,* but I said, "I didn't ask you to believe it, I asked you to assume you believed it so that you would understand why someone who did believe would give two years of his or her life."

With that, he folded up his lap-top computer and headed for the door. I couldn't resist one more comment. I concluded as I shook his hand, "Isn't it interesting that all of the attributes and fruits of our church about which you have expressed great admiration thus sprang forth out of a fabrication or imagination?"

He stopped, thought a moment, unpacked his computer, and started typing something. I almost shudder to think now how I was quoted. He never sent me a copy.

It is difficult to understand the phenomenon of the growth of the kingdom without knowing and understanding ancient and modern scripture. It is impossible to understand a testimony if you have never had one. The world equates belief with spiritual witness (testimony). They are as different as a theory is from a fact.

A recent column in the *Dallas Morning News,* entitled "Liberal Proposals Don't Seem to Draw Seekers To Religion," sheds some light on why people are becoming disenchanted with their current religions. Indirectly, this article, which describes a Protestant church that I won't mention by name, gives some intellectual reasons why our church is attractive to honest seekers of truth:

> Twenty-five years ago, Time magazine created a stir by asking on its cover, "Is God dead?" The debate was whether there is a God, whether he was sleeping through this century, whether anybody cared.
>
> This month, Time devoted a half-dozen pages to the question of evil—does it exist? Is there more now than five years ago, or five centuries? Time didn't resolve the theological issue, but it was refreshing to see a moral subject more complex than Bart Simpson T-shirts and Madonna videos on the cover of a news magazine.
>
> Other events in the news indicated that religion is not only alive, but in a state of tremendous ferment. The [Protestant church] was in knots and in the headlines, as leaders argued whether to reject traditional sexual

ethics and accept homosexuality, premarital sex and extramarital sex into the church teachings. The elders voted nay, but not before losing some credibility over the public fight. Despite the overwhelming vote against the changes in the end, the impression was of a denomination that was not sure who it was or what it believed in. . . .

One of the unsettling aspects of the . . . family fight was that it seemed fueled in part by the recognition that the denomination was losing numbers and might need to refashion its beliefs to attract more people. Church leaders expressed concern that the denomination had declined by a half a million members in the last 20 years. But adopting a HyperMart theology merely to draw crowds — something marked down for everybody! — seemed to have more to do with marketing than conscience. Ironically, the fastest-growing faiths are not those that airbrush the sin out of their views, but those with strict prescriptions for living. . . .

Are the old-line denominations losing their flocks because they are asking too little rather than too much? There is evidence every day of a surge of interest in religion. . . .

The . . . reformers may be right that there is a large segment of the American public that is practicing a more relaxed moral code. A book published this spring [1992], "The Day America Told the Truth," claims that its national survey showed that:

• A third of the men and women surveyed confessed to having at least one affair.

• Only 13 percent of Americans believed in the Ten Commandments.

• Ninety-one percent said they lie regularly; 40 percent admit they lie to their spouses.

• One-third of AIDS carriers had not told their spouses or lovers of their disease.

But the poll also showed 90 percent of Americans

say they believe in God. And indeed, another national survey released this spring by City University of New York showed nine in 10 Americans identify with a religious denomination, be it Lutheran, Mormon, Scientologist or Rastafarian. . . .

So we have a salad bar of religions, with millions of people trying to find answers, comfort, directions for living. Where [the Protestant denomination] seemed to misjudge the trend was that generally people want their religion to be better than they are. The . . . reformers tried to refashion their doctrine to fit the polls showing moral lassitude. This would be like diluting our nation's laws to match the personal integrity of our lawmakers. The idea, after all, is to reach for the heavens, not settle for the morals of the guy next door.

I found this column to be refreshing and insightful. I believe, in spite of the moral decadence all around us, that there is a religious renaissance going on. Those who have learned the hard way are looking for truth. Young singles and couples, for example, are joining The Church of Jesus Christ of Latter-day Saints in increasing numbers. They are looking for absolute truths.

The Church is growing very rapidly and yet we know through prophecy that our numbers will always be few. Nephi wrote: "It came to pass that I beheld the church of the Lamb of God, and its numbers were few, because of the wickedness and abominations of the whore who sat upon many waters; nevertheless, I beheld that the church of the Lamb, who were the saints of God, were also upon all the face of the earth; and their dominions upon the face of the earth were small, because of the wickedness of the great whore whom I saw." (1 Nephi 14:12.)

We should not let this scripture blunt our enthusiasm,

excitement, or efforts in missionary work. In a world of ten billion, one billion members would still be few. Each individual is precious in the sight of God, and our excitement should not wane whether we are a church of ten million or three hundred million.

The greatest growth we see in the Church in recent years is occurring in countries where there is much poverty. This shouldn't surprise us because this has always been the case. The Lord loves the poor because their humility fine-tunes their ears to hear and their hearts to accept the gospel. In the Book of Mormon Alma tells about the missionaries who went to preach among the Zoramites:

> And it came to pass that after much labor among them, [the missionaries] began to have success among the poor class of people; for behold, they were cast out of the synagogues because of the coarseness of their apparel — therefore they were not permitted to enter into their synagogues to worship God, being esteemed as filthiness; therefore they were poor; yea, they were esteemed by their brethren as dross; therefore they were poor as to things of the world; and also they were poor in heart.
>
> Now, as Alma was teaching and speaking unto the people upon the hill Onidah, there came a great multitude unto him, who were those of whom we have been speaking, of whom were poor in heart, because of their poverty as to the things of the world.
>
> And they came unto Alma; and the one who was the foremost among them said unto him: Behold, what shall these my brethren do, for they are despised of all men because of their poverty, yea, and more especially by our priests; for they have cast us out of our synagogues which we have labored abundantly to build with our own hands; and they have cast us out because of

our exceeding poverty; and we have no place to worship our God; and behold, what shall we do?

And now when Alma heard this, he turned him about, his face immediately towards him, and he beheld with great joy; for he beheld that their afflictions had truly humbled them, and that they were in a preparation to hear the word. (Alma 32:2–6.)

In modern scripture, we read, "The poor and the meek shall have the gospel preached unto them, and they shall be looking forth for the time of my coming." (D&C 35:15.) Therefore, "Blessed are the poor who are pure in heart, whose hearts are broken, and whose spirits are contrite, for they shall see the kingdom of God coming in power and great glory unto their deliverance; for the fatness of the earth shall be theirs." (D&C 56:18.)

Elder Augusto A. Lim of the Second Quorum of the Seventy recently testified of the growth of the Church in the Philippines and gave his opinion as to the reason for that growth:

> We are often asked the reasons behind this phenomenal growth in membership. I could only venture some opinions: first, that being perhaps the only Christian country in Asia for many centuries now had prepared the people for the coming of the gospel. That the Philippines, being considered the third largest English-speaking country in the world, certainly made it easier for people to understand the message of the gospel and is the reason for the fast development of the leadership skills of its members.
>
> But more important is the humble nature of the people and their dependence on the Lord for the things they stand in need of, making them receptive to the prompting of the Spirit. Because of economic difficulties

experienced in the Philippines, the gospel is the answer, and rightly so, to the people's prayer for a better way of life. As a result of the gospel-centered lives of many Latter-day Saints, people around them see changes in their lives that in turn give them hope. Member families may still live in humble homes with dirt or bamboo floors and walls, but because of their positive response to the gospel plan, and through their obedience to the Lord's commandments, they receive the promised blessings and, as a result, people see the changes in these families who are now living in a more sanitary condition, are healthier, more educated, always ready and delighted to help others, grateful for what they have, no matter how humble, and generally happier. They have obeyed the Lord's counsel to "learn of me, and listen to my words; walk in the meekness of my Spirit, and you shall have peace in me." (D&C 19:23.) Generally, however, the faith, devotion, and living of correct gospel principles by the members have improved their lives not only spiritually but also temporally, for did not the Lord say that the "willing and obedient shall eat the good of the land of Zion in these last days"? (D&C 64:34.) (*Ensign*, November 1992, p. 83.)

Today such a revival is taking place in the hearts of many people throughout the world!

4

Some Success Stories

May I now introduce to you some friends of mine, true
Saints, who live in Africa and some heartwarming experiences I have had with them. These are individuals whom
the Lord knows and loves; they are not just statistics of
reported growth. Similar stories could be reported in other
so-called "developing countries" where people are humble
and anxious to hear the word of the Lord.

Let me say at the outset that my experience is limited
on the subject. Many of my brethren have spent years
serving members of the Church in Africa and would be
more qualified than I to address the subject; my experience
consists of visiting for two weeks a year for about seven
years. I would also say that we are not without our problems in Africa. Nevertheless, I have made some acquain-
tances who have made lasting impressions on me and
provide examples of pure hearts.

There is a pentecostal spirit of New Testament proportions among these peoples. They have relatively nothing of temporal value, and yet they have everything of eternal importance.

Great numbers of converts have come into the Church in Africa. On my first visit I asked each missionary couple, "Are they really converted?" I wondered if the Joseph Smith experience was just another story that was easy for them to believe since it was reasonably consistent with some of their own supernatural beliefs. When I found myself alone with a missionary couple, I would say, "We're alone now; you can tell me the real story. Do they have strong testimonies?"

I must have asked the question of one missionary couple one too many times, because they finally replied, "Why don't you come to church with us tomorrow to a remote branch and draw your own conclusion?"

The branch to which they were referring was one where the whole village of 150 people had come into the Church at once. Not one person in the congregation had been a member for more than six months. We drove up in a four-wheel-drive vehicle and then walked to the modest chapel. There I observed a beautiful testimony meeting. I saw young Aaronic Priesthood men bless and pass the sacrament with reverence we would all do well to emulate. I saw a district president gently correct little technicalities when not all the right words were used in the confirmation of a new member of the Church. I sat in priesthood quorum meeting where there were only three or four manuals for twenty prospective elders. Because of the humidity and the heavy usage, the books were coming apart. However, every page was handled as if it were scripture or, a more apt comparison, a page from the golden plates themselves.

Most important, in this branch I felt a great, powerful spirit. My turmoil was ended.

A young man fifteen years of age caught my eye because he was leading the Primary children in singing "I Am a Child of God." I struck up a conversation, and when I returned home, I received a letter from him. Keep in mind this young man had been a member of the Church for only six months. See if you don't recognize the same devotion and commitment that we read about in connection with our early pioneer forefathers.

"Dear Bishop," he began, "Love and peace in Jesus name abide with you. It has taken quite a long time since you came to our branch. It was a joyous day and we would like to cherish your smiling face once more. How are things moving in the General Authorities of the Church and its administration? I know you have been doing your best for our branch. Our branch in the Aba District is increasing and progressing and we hope to become more than a branch someday."

As I read these words, I asked myself, Why does a fifteen-year-old boy care whether he is in a ward or a branch? After being in the Church for only six months, how does he even know the difference? His letter continues:

"Your true, heartwarming, strong testimonies which you gave in our branch are still alive. I enjoyed listening to your voice in the cassette when you were speaking at a conference meeting about the welfare program. I know your testimonies are true."

Here is a young man who has access to general conference tapes. Imagine a fifteen-year-old boy being more excited about conference tapes arriving than about the newest heavy-metal music cassette. Just to make sure I would know he wasn't putting me on, he told me what I had talked about! Then he went on:

"To introduce myself. I am Samuel, the second son of the branch president. I am a fifteen-year-old boy, a teacher in the Aaronic Priesthood and the branch investigator's teacher. I'm the secretary in the young adult program and one of the song leaders in our branch. I was the boy, if you remember, who picked your pen and returned it when you left it with me after giving me your address at our branch. Could you remember when you remarked that I have acted like Mormons?"

I had told him he acted like a young man who had been a member of the Church all of his life rather than for just a few months. He took my comment as the ultimate compliment.

"How is our president, seer, and revelator, Prophet Ezra Taft Benson? I know the Lord is improving his health condition and increasing his life span. Next time you feel his hands, tell him that I love him so much. Also ask him to remember me as he prays in the holy temple. Inform him I need his blessings to progress in my studies and pass my examinations. The Lord who has chosen him will help him magnify his callings very well in this dispensation of fulness of time. I pray the Lord will guide you to deliver my message to him."

What beautiful, simple faith! I shared this letter with President Benson. He was touched, and we put Samuel's name on the prayer roll in the temple.

"When are we going to have a stake in my country?" Samuel asked. "I will like us to have a stake here in my country and missionaries to live with us so as to meet the demands of the growing Church, talk to the Prophet about this issue."

In addition to his faith, Samuel also has a can-do attitude. It is worth noting that his branch is now a ward, and the Aba District has now become two stakes.

"I very much like to open contact with you and your family and would like you to introduce me to your family members. I will meet you again and I know that.

"May God bless the Church in general and your family in particular is my prayer. Please write to me soonest. Yours faithfully, Samuel."

A couple of years later, I was in Africa again and tried to find Samuel. Just before I left for the airport to come home, I talked to a man who was his home teacher. He told me that Samuel was now living on his own, working and going to school. On the way to the airport, I wrote Samuel a note, explaining how I had tried to find him and hoped all was well. In response, I received a letter from which the following are excerpts:

> Dear Beloved Bishop,
>
> It has been quite a long time now since I have written you, but I am with you in spirit and quite often I remember you in my prayers.
>
> It was a very sad moment when I met the assistant director of seminary at the stake centre. He told me, "Bishop Pace came to Nigeria and he very much wanted to see you but you were not at home." It pained me in the heart so much that I missed you that day in the Sunday School, sacrament meeting, and quorum I kept remembering you. It would have been an opportunity to shake your hands, see your smiling face and talk to you once more. If it had occurred to me, I would have postponed my journey because I had prayed to see you

but all the same, God has a way of doing his own thing, I know that.

Bishop, this letter is not enough to contain my heart now, I will write to you again. I still remember the first day we met in our branch. After the meeting I requested your address. You were very kind to give me your address and you forgot your beautiful writing pen with me. I picked it up and ran and gave it to you. How you smiled and said to me "You are a good Mormon." That day was wonderful.

I like to tell you that I love you, and the church as a whole. Ezra Taft Benson is a true prophet of God. May our Heavenly Father continue to guide and protect you and your family till we meet again here or in the celestial kingdom in Christ, amen.

Samuel

The next year we made a connection. Samuel is now waiting for his brother to return from a mission so that he may go. He talks about it, dreams about it, and lives completely worthy of it.

Another inspiring example comes from Ghana. In 1989, the Ghanaian government froze the activities of the Church. This meant, among other things, that all North Americans left, chapels were taken over by the government, and it became against the law to congregate. The reason for this was basically that because the Church had grown very rapidly, local ministers had become alarmed, pressure had been placed on the government, misunderstandings had arisen, and a hasty decision had been made. I had been there just a few months prior to the freeze and had met many wonderful Saints. Representative of them was a young priest named Michael. He wrote me a letter approximately six months after the freeze took effect and told me about the impact it had on him. His letter is dated Christmas Eve, 1989. Some excerpts follow:

Dear Bishop Pace,

I am very glad to write you this humble letter. My name is Michael, I have black hair, black eyes, and fair in complexion.

Now, if I could remember you, you came to Ghana sometime ago and visited our branch. You took a lot of pictures that day and if you have got those of the priest, I am the boy wearing the black suit with an usher tag.

I think you know what has happened in Ghana, but all the same I can assure you that it has been a blessing. It is good to give you my version of the story. It all happened on the 14th of June 1989. It was on Wednesday. I had just returned from school for holidays, and I was preparing myself for choir practice which I enjoy very much.

So, it came to pass that I was resting in my father's car when he called, "Michael! Have you heard what has happened?" I said, "No," he then went on to tell me that the government has frozen the activities of the church. From this, I just got up and said, "They are joking, for no power on this earth can stop this church."

From that time onwards in the newspapers, and news bulletins and even in town it was a topic for discussion. We had two sides: those against and those in favour. In one occasion, a riot broke out between a member of a pentecostal church and a non-church goer. According to the pentecostal man, he was happy that the church's activities had been frozen and this was the reply he got from the other man: "Mr., don't be happy. I know this church very well, I have been to Britain so I know what the church stands for. It is the only true church on earth, and I tell you that I will be the first person to be baptized when their activity is unfrozen." Bishop, these are the words of a nonmember. Due to what has happened, people have got to know about the church.

In my high school, on a Sunday, some students came to me and said brother Michael, you are a Mormon?

I said, "Yes," they then said tell us more about this church and the Book of Mormon. After hearing this, I said to myself, "This is the hour." So I explained everything to them and after knowing something about the church, they became happy. Many people have been inquiring about the church and after telling them something they pledge to join the church when it starts to operate again.

Bishop, all members here in our branch greet you and your family. We like to tell you that our faith is now even stronger than before, we are praying and waiting patiently for the day we will return.

I was so touched and impressed by this letter that I immediately wrote to Michael. Soon I received a reply, which was written when the Church had been closed in Ghana for over nine months. He began:

"Dear Bishop Pace, I was very grateful and humble when I received your letter dated 21 January 1990. A young boy and coming from a poor home was not expecting this sort of respect. My parents were filled with tears of joy when they heard that you have written. As I am now writing, in the dormitory of my school, I am in deep humility with tears all over my eyes."

As I read this, I realized that the humble tears shed had little to do with Bishop Pace, but more with the overwhelming desire to be in complete contact with the Brethren and to be able to have the kingdom continue to grow in his land. His letter continued:

For I feel for the church and its activities, I feel for

the voice of the prophet and all general authorities. But all is not lost yet. For I know that one day we shall meet again.

Concerning the members, most families hold their sacrament meetings and family home evenings but as you would expect, unfortunately, some have fallen. We usually pay frequent visits to members to strengthen their faith in the gospel due to rising persecutions especially from other churches.

Bishop, I attend a Catholic school where all go to worship as the Catholics do. One Sunday, a Catholic priest was invited to come and preach, but in his preaching he totally condemned the "Mormons." I was there and heard it which immediately strengthened my faith. After closing, I left the church laughing and saying, "Lord forgive him, for he does not know what he is doing." To tell you the honest truth, I know that the church is true and nothing can separate me and my family from it.

In my letter I had asked Michael what message he would like me to deliver at a reunion of the missionary couples who had served in Ghana. He wrote:

This is my message for the returned missionaries and also that we in Ghana know perfectly well that one day we will resume activities in unity and love to build Zion for as one prophet said, the church is moving according to the timetable of heaven. But tell them that they should be of good cheer and work hard for he who endures to the end shall be saved.

I would like to end with a quotation I usually share with my family members to strengthen ourselves and this can be found in D&C 122:6–7 which says:

"If thou art accused with all manner of false accusation: if thine enemies fall upon thee: if they tear thee from the society of thy father and mother and brethren and sisters. . . . if thy

enemies prowl around thee like wolves for the blood of the Lamb . . . even if the very jaws of hell shall gape open the mouth wide after thee, know thou my son that all these things shall give thee experience and shall be for thy good."

This is what I leave with you, hoping to get your reply very soon in the hallowed name of our Lord and Saviour Jesus Christ. Amen.

Your Son, Michael

Approximately one year after the return of the Church to Ghana, Michael was called to serve a mission in his country. Soon afterwards he wrote me the following letter:

Aloha Bishop,

It is almost impossible to express one's joy due to righteous living and I am happy to say this is my condition as of now. "No greater joy can come to man than carrying the gospel to all nations, kindred, tongue, and people!"

Bishop, the tall and short of the whole matter is that your son and friend Michael is now a full-time missionary of no other church but The Church of Jesus Christ of Latter-day Saints. Please allow me to start from the scratch. It so happened, that one day after getting up from bed, I got to my desk and started studying the scriptures. In a nutshell it talked about choosing mission when mission clashes with school. During that very day the mission president's assistants were here. They called me and their message was, "try and get onto the mission field." In the evening, after Daddy had arrived from work he called me and asked, "When are you going on a mission?" Without hesitation, I answered, "Now!" Because I came to realize that if I disobey the three calls the Lord has given to me that very day and continue my education as was planned, I was going to regret later in my life.

Although I'm only three-weeks old a lot has been

achieved in terms of the organized discussions. Also my testimony about the church has increased and I hope to work tirelessly for me to gain the necessary blessings. I actually studied the scriptures at home, prayed, fasted and did everything worthy of a Latter-day Saint but in doing all these things I did not feel the Spirit and the power of the holy priesthood as I am doing now in the mission field. As a result I bear my humble testimony that the *priesthood is alive!*

I know of a surety, that I am engaged in a glorious cause which will better my life first and foremost, than others. And this is my glory that I would be an instrument in the hands of God to bring some soul to repentance and this is also my joy.

Yours faithfully, Elder Michael

When I returned to Ghana a few months after the freeze was lifted, I wondered how the few thousand Saints there could have survived with their tender roots, without being connected by an umbilical cord to Salt Lake City. This question was answered promptly and convincingly.

When I went back to the same branch—Michael's branch—that I had visited prior to the freeze, the first thing I noticed was that the members had painted the rented facility where they met. Although it was a very modest, humble building, they had done all they could do to make it acceptable to the Lord.

The next thing I noticed was that the congregation was larger than it had been two years earlier. There were more than twenty people in the investigator class. Michael was my host and interpreted for me. He was especially excited to introduce me to two young men who had been among the students who had surrounded him that day in school when he was asked, "Are you a Mormon?" They were now excited investigators of the Church.

It is significant to note that within six months after the freeze was lifted, Elders Boyd K. Packer and James E. Faust of the Council of the Twelve organized the first two stakes of Zion in Ghana. The congregation where I met Michael is now a ward. Some time later my wife and I visited there again and saw that ground had been broken for a new chapel. The members' plea to us to take back to the Brethren was, "When will we have a temple?"

One of the most inspiring experiences of my life occurred the first time I went to Ghana after the Church had again received permission to be there. When the governmental edict had come for the Church to leave, more than seventy Ghanaian elders and sisters were serving full-time missions in their country, and immediately their missions were over. A few of them were thrown in jail for several days. All of them eventually returned to their homes to take up their lives of school, work, and, in some cases, dating.

Eighteen months later, again without notice, the Church was back. These missionaries were all contacted to see if they wanted to finish their missions. I was privileged to sit in on several of those interviews. As our party pulled up to the chapel at Cape Coast, excitement was in the air. The young men and women were experiencing something that was a cross between a missionary reunion and a spiritual revival. I will share with you a few of our experiences in those interviews.

At the time of the freeze, the first elder we talked to still had eighteen months left to serve. He went to live with his family in Liberia, where his family was active in the Church. When civil unrest and violence broke out in that country, the family managed to escape unharmed and go to Ghana. When asked if he understood and was living the law of chastity, he assured us that he was and explained, "You don't do certain things with women that are reserved for marriage." Then he told us, "I want to continue to serve." He was worthy and anxious to resume his mission even though his life had just settled down.

The next elder, the only member of the Church in his family, also had eighteen months left of his mission. His brother had offered to send him enough money to go to London to find a job and attend school. We asked him to express his testimony. He said, "When I used to read the Bible, I read it more like a story book. After I joined the Church, I have now begun to ponder every word. When I heard about the Church, I felt like I had come home. I felt joy which I had never really felt before. I don't want to do anything wrong to spoil the joy I feel. I always knew that the Church would come back because I felt it in my heart. I have written to my brother and asked if he will consider keeping the offer open for eighteen months."

The next young man was twelve years old when he joined the Church, making him one of the early members of the Church in Ghana. During the freeze, he often wore his missionary badge so that people would ask him questions, giving him an opportunity to defend the Church and explain what it really is. He was also one of the elders thrown into jail at the beginning of the freeze.

Another elder had acquired a taxi during the freeze, and his family and some members of the branch were counseling him not to return to his mission because he would lose it. He told us, "Heavenly Father helped me get this taxi. If I finish my commitment to him, he is very capable of getting me another car when I get back if that is what he wants me to do."

Next we interviewed a sister who had twelve months left of her mission. She had been living with her sister before her mission, and after the Church activities were frozen, she was persecuted harshly by family members and others in her village. She had some concern about returning to the mission field for fear that after her mission she would receive the same treatment. When asked if she had been living the standards of the Church, she said she had except for one thing: "I was sick. The doctor recommended for my low blood pressure that I have a little bit of alcohol each day. I did that for a few days and then decided that I would rather have low blood pressure than break the Word of Wisdom, so I stopped taking it. Am I still worthy to serve?"

Many more examples could be given. In the Church we have talked a lot lately about getting back to basics. These people and many others I have met are living the basics. I see in them the epitome of the Lord's counsel to become "as a child, submissive, meek, humble, patient, full of love, willing to submit to all things which the Lord seeth fit to inflict upon him, even as a child doth submit to his father." (Mosiah 3:19.) We have been told that "little children do have words given unto them many times, which confound the wise and the learned." (Alma 32:23.)

"And it came to pass that [Jesus] did teach and minister unto the children of the multitude of whom hath been spoken, and he did loose their tongues, and they did speak unto their fathers great and marvelous things, even greater than he had revealed unto the people; and he loosed their tongues that they could utter." (3 Nephi 26:14.)

"I am filled with charity, which is everlasting love; wherefore, all children are alike unto me; wherefore, I love little children with a perfect love; and they are all alike and partakers of salvation." (Moroni 8:17.)

I am grateful for the example I have seen in the Saints in Africa who have shown me what becoming "as a child" means. It does not mean childish, but childlike. There the gospel is taught and lived in simplicity.

Other countries could have been used as examples because we see this spirit everywhere when people are humble and are doing everything possible to live the gospel and build the kingdom. They have nothing and yet they have everything.

When are we going to follow their example? When are we going to get on the train and stay on?

When I was in Primary, I used to observe missionaries giving their reports in sacrament meeting and I'd think, *I can't wait until I have the priesthood so I can have spiritual experiences like that.* When I was a deacon, I'd think, *I can't wait until I get the Melchizedek Priesthood so I can have spiritual experiences like that.* When I was finally old enough to go on a mission, I couldn't wait to receive my mission call. Then I couldn't wait to go to the mission home so I could have spiritual experiences. At the mission home, I couldn't wait to get on the train that would take me to Boston where I could begin my mission and have spiritual experiences. Guess what! When I got off the train in Boston, I was the same guy who had stepped on the train in Salt Lake City.

Only we hold ourselves back from having spiritual experiences. We need to do whatever is necessary to bring such experiences into our lives and not wait for someone or something to bring them to us. Great and marvelous things are coming our way as we move into the latter part of the dispensation of the fulness of times. We will have special experiences that will make our testimonies soar, but we must develop wings here and now.

5

Putting on
the Full Armor

The last days contain a full spectrum of life's conditions. We truly live in the best of times and the worst of times. To some, the events unfolding in the world today are frightening. This is not a time to panic, but it is definitely a time to prepare.

The preparation of which I speak is not just for self-defense but also to enable each of us to be more useful to the Lord in the building of his kingdom in the last days. The same things that are a shield and protection in the last days can also be a sword and plowshare.

What can we do to better prepare ourselves for that which is at our doorstep? It is simple. We need to get back to basics and learn obedience. The Lord has told us, "My people must needs be chastened until they learn obedience, if it must needs be, by the things which they suffer." (D&C 105:6.)

When we are obedient, we follow the first principles of the gospel and place our faith in our Lord and Savior, repent of our sins, are baptized, and receive the Holy Ghost to guide us. We read and ponder the scriptures, pray for direction in our lives, and look for ways to help others who are going through difficult times. We share the gospel with people living on earth and make it possible for saving ordinances to be performed for those who have passed beyond the veil.

In general conference and on many other occasions we are taught by the Lord's anointed servants. These prophets, seers, and revelators receive revelation, relative to the kingdom, to which their mantle entitles them. We follow the Brethren. Finally, we prepare ourselves to receive an endowment in the temple. If we remain faithful, this endowment literally gives us additional power to overcome the sins of the world and "stand in holy places." (D&C 45:32.)

"There is none other place appointed than that which I have appointed; neither shall there be any other place appointed than that which I have appointed, for the work of the gathering of my saints. . . . Behold, it is my will, that all they who call on my name, and worship me according to mine everlasting gospel, should gather together, and stand in holy places. . . . That the work of the gathering together of my saints may continue, that I may build them up unto my name upon holy places; for the time of harvest is come, and my word must needs be fulfilled." (D&C 101:20, 22, 64.)

What does it mean to stand in holy places? It certainly means more than having our names recorded as members of particular stakes of Zion. To be safe and to be useful to the Lord, we must be members in good standing. We must be obedient in order that we can enjoy the protection of the full armor of God.

Elder Ezra Taft Benson said, "Certainly spirituality is the foundation upon which any battle against sin and tyranny must be waged. And because this is basically the struggle of the forces of Christ versus Antichrist, it is imperative that our people be in tune with the supreme leader of freedom, the Lord our God. And men only stay in tune when their lives are in harmony with God, for apart from God we cannot succeed, but as a partner with God, we cannot fail. We must be in the amoral and immoral world, but not of it." (Conference Report, April 1967, p. 60.)

According to President Marion G. Romney,

> Spirituality comes by faith, repentance, baptism, and reception of the Holy Ghost. One who has the companionship of the Holy Ghost is in harmony with God. He is, therefore, spiritual. Spirituality is sustained by so living as to keep that companionship.
>
> A sure way for us to do this is to learn what our duties are and perform them. They include obeying the first and second great commandments: "Thou shalt love the Lord thy God with all thy heart, and with all thy soul, and with all thy mind" and "Thou shalt love thy neighbour as thyself" (Matt. 22:37, 39). They also include obedience to the Ten Commandments and the Sermon on the Mount, implementing the Articles of Faith, and prayer. . . .
>
> Spirituality, brothers and sisters, will come to all who will follow this pattern, for the Lord himself has said: "It shall come to pass that every soul who forsaketh his sins and cometh unto me, and calleth on my name, and obeyeth my voice, and keepeth my commandments,

shall see my face and know that I am." (D&C 93:1.) (Conference Report, October 1979, pp. 20, 23.)

Elder Neal A. Maxwell told us our obedience to the Lord and his leaders will be as important to us as was the obedience of the children of Israel to Moses: "Remember how, with Pharaoh's angry army in hot pursuit, ancient Israel aligned themselves with the Lord's instructions? Moses stretched forth his hand and the Red Sea parted. With towering walls of water on each side, Israel walked through the narrow passage obediently, and no doubt quickly! There were no warnings about conforming on that day!

"There are passages ahead which will require similar obedience, as prophets lead the 'men [and women] of Christ' in a straight and narrow course. Becoming more like Jesus in thought and behavior is not grinding and repressing, but emancipating and discovering! Unorthodoxy in behavior and intellect is just the opposite." (*Ensign*, November 1992, p. 67.)

One of the misconceptions our young people seem to have is that commandments are given to prevent them from having fun. Commandments aren't given just to keep us from suffering after we die, but to provide a full, rewarding, and happy earth life. On the wall of our kitchen is a picture of a hen talking to her chicks. The caption reads, "Because I'm the mommy, that's why."

From parents, Church leaders, seminary teachers, and others, youth hear "Don't do this" and "Don't do that." Lists of do's and don'ts appear in the scriptures. I've always been one who wants to know why. Parents can't always explain why, and often children wouldn't understand if they were given the reason. Certainly this is true on some issues. However, there are good, logical, and spiritual reasons for doing the things we are asked or commanded to do. The Lord gave the reason for sacrifice to Adam when he knew Adam would understand and appreciate it. We too can receive answers to our questions when we are worthy and ready.

Some people feel they must always understand the why of a commandment before they obey. Hugh Nibley gave some sound reasoning on those commandments or ordinances we may not fully understand:

> When one goes to train with a master, not merely with the object of serving time for a certificate as in our modern "character factories," but in order to learn all the master has to teach and to become as far as possible perfect in an art, a science, or a craft, the first and all-important step is to establish a condition of complete trust between the master and the disciple. The candidate must by sure tests show his implicit faith and unhesitating obedience to every command in every situation. Soon enough he will understand *why* he must take a seemingly absurd position or perform some apparently meaningless operation; but unless and until he does the thing and does it entirely on faith and does it with a will, he will never come to that understanding, worlds without end.
>
> There are many things that can only be explained after they are done, and then the explanation of what seemed so arbitrary and mysterious usually turns out to be extremely obvious and natural. We are required, for example, to use oil in some of the ordinances of the Church, and water in others. If you ask me why, I will answer, "I know not, save that the Lord hath commanded" (Moses 5:6). That is reason enough. It does not follow that these things have no real purpose aside

from the symbolic and disciplinary: A small child uses soap on faith—a mere act of obedience, we might say, with the soap as a symbol of cleanliness, but actually it goes much further than that; the soap performs a real function which the child does not understand. I doubt not that when we know the reason for some of the things we do now on faith, the practical value of the actions will be so plain that we will wonder how we could have missed it, and then we shall be heartily glad that we did what we were told to do. Meantime the Lord advises us in these things, and it is up to us to trust his judgment. If the primary purpose of our being on earth is to be tested, and the first thing to be tested is our faith and obedience, it is foolish to ask for a full explanation before we will move a muscle. (*The World and the Prophets* [Salt Lake City: Deseret Book Company, and Provo: Foundation for Ancient Research and Mormon Studies, 1987], pp. 148–49.)

We don't know exactly how obedience will save us from the events of the future. However, we do know from scriptural accounts that obedience has saved others in their tribulation. This was effectively pointed out by Elder Bruce R. McConkie:

We can rest assured that if we have done all in our power to prepare for whatever lies ahead, [God] will then help us with whatever else we need.

He rained manna from heaven upon all Israel, six days each week for forty years, lest they perish for want of bread, but the manna ceased on the morrow after they ate of the parched corn of Canaan. Then they were required to supply their own food. (See Exod. 16:3–4, 35.)

During forty years in the wilderness the clothes worn by all Israel waxed not old and their shoes wore not out, but when they entered their promised land, then the

Lord required them to provide their own wearing apparel. (See Deut. 29:5.)

When there was a famine in the land, at Elijah's word, a certain barrel of meal did not waste, and a certain cruse of oil did not fail, until the Lord sent again rain on the earth. And it is worthy of note, as Jesus said, that though there were many widows in Israel, unto one only was Elijah sent. (See 1 Kings 17:10–16.)

We do not say that all of the Saints will be spared and saved from the coming day of desolation. But we do say there is no promise of safety and no promise of security except for those who love the Lord and who are seeking to do all that he commands. It may be, for instance, that nothing except the power of faith and the authority of the priesthood can save individuals and congregations from the atomic holocausts that surely shall be. (Conference Report, April 1979, p. 133.)

A similar warning on war was given 130 years ago by President George Q. Cannon. He declared, "War is one of the scourges which man, by his sinfulness, has brought upon himself. There is one way—and but one way—to avert it and that is for the people to obey God's commands, through whose power alone can this and other threatened evils be stayed. This is too simple for the great men of the earth to believe. . . . They view such a proposition as ridiculous and treat it with contempt, practically asserting by their actions that they consider their wisdom and plans as being infinitely superior to the Lord's. The day will come when they will see their folly and be constrained to acknowledge it; but in the most of instances it will be when they will not have the power to avail themselves of the knowledge." (*Gospel Truth*, p. 45.)

Recently, Elder M. Russell Ballard reminded the Saints, "The Lord is in control. He knows the end from the beginning. He has given us adequate instruction that, if followed, will see us safely through any crisis. His purposes will be fulfilled, and someday we will understand the eternal reasons for all of these events. Therefore, today we must be careful to not overreact, nor should we be caught up in extreme preparations, but what we must do is keep the commandments of God and never lose hope! . . . Our Heavenly Father is aware of us, individually and collectively. He understands the spiritual, physical, and emotional difficulties we face in the world today. In fact, they are all part of His plan for our eternal growth and development. And His promise to us is sure: 'He that endureth in faith and doeth my will, the same shall overcome.' (D&C 63:20.)" (*Ensign*, November 1992, pp. 32–33.)

Elder Dean L. Larsen of the First Quorum of the Seventy has also spoken on the subject of obedience:

> The Lord has demonstrated throughout the generations that when the inhabitants of the earth remember him and are obedient to his direction, he will bless them not only with spiritual blessings, but with material abundance as well. . . .
>
> Perhaps the greatest tragedies of all time have occurred when people have received the promised blessings of the Lord and then have forgotten the source of their good life. . . . It is one thing to look back upon the events of history. It is another to regard our own time. We have the Lord's assurance that he will bless and prosper his people if they will keep his commandments and remember to look to him as the source of their blessings.
>
> On the other hand, we must not forget that these blessings are conditional. As King Limhi warned his people, "For behold, the Lord hath said: I will not succor my people in the day of their transgression; but I will

hedge up their ways that they prosper not; and their doings shall be as a stumbling block before them." (Mosiah 7:29.) . . . As the world continues to ripen in iniquity, our lives of necessity must become increasingly different from the world and its standard. It will be a great challenge for us. We must be better than we have ever been before. As we succeed, we have the sure promise of the Lord that he will prosper us in every way necessary for our well-being. (*Ensign,* November 1992, pp. 40, 42.)

President Howard W. Hunter encourages us to place our trust in the Savior, obey His will, and become as He is, and promises safety to those who do so:

Let me recall one of the great stories of Christ's triumph over that which seems to test us and try us and bring fear to our hearts. As Christ's disciples had set out on one of their frequent journeys across the Sea of Galilee, the night was dark and the elements were strong and contrary. The waves were boisterous and the wind was bold, and these mortal, frail men were frightened. Unfortunately there was no one with them to calm and save them, for Jesus had been left alone upon the shore.

As always, he was watching over them. He loved them and cared for them. In their moment of greatest extremity they looked and saw in the darkness an image in a fluttering robe, walking toward them on the ridges of the sea. They cried out in terror at the sight, thinking that it was a phantom that walked upon the waves. And through the storm and darkness to them—as so often to us, when, amid the darknesses of life, the ocean seems so great and our little boats so small—there came the ultimate and reassuring voice of peace with this simple declaration, "It is I; be not afraid." Peter exclaimed, "Lord, if it be thou, bid me come unto thee on the water."

And Christ's answer to him was the same as to all of us: "Come."

Peter sprang over the vessel's side and into the troubled waves, and while his eyes were fixed upon the Lord, the wind might toss his hair and the spray might drench his robes, but all was well. Only when with wavering faith he removed his glance from the Master to look at the furious waves and the black gulf beneath him, only then did he begin to sink. Again, like most of us, he cried, "Lord, save me." Nor did Jesus fail him. He stretched out his hand and grasped the drowning disciple with the gentle rebuke, "O thou of little faith, why didst thou doubt?"

Then safely aboard their little craft, they saw the wind fall and the crash of the waves become a ripple. Soon they were at their haven, their safe port, where all would one day hope to be. The crew as well as his disciples were filled with deep amazement. Some of them addressed him by a title which I declare today: "Truly thou art the Son of God." (Adapted from Farrar, *The Life of Christ,* pp. 310–13; see Matt. 14:22–33.)

It is my firm belief that if as individual people, as families, communities, and nations, we could, like Peter, fix our eyes on Jesus, we too might walk triumphantly over "the swelling waves of disbelief" and remain "unterrified amid the rising winds of doubt." But if we turn away our eyes from him in whom we must believe, as it is so easy to do and the world is so much tempted to do, if we look to the power and fury of those terrible and destructive elements around us rather than to him who can help and save us, then we shall inevitably sink in a sea of conflict and sorrow and despair. (*Ensign,* November 1992, p. 19.)

It is time for us to put on the full armor of God by keeping his commandments. The woods are too dangerous without our armor. We are literally in a war with Lucifer, and it is time to stop giving him the home-court advantage. We simply cannot continue to expect the Lord's protection when we take the commandments lightly. Even the Savior is bound by absolute truth. The truth is: "There is a law, irrevocably decreed in heaven before the foundations of this world, upon which all blessings are predicated — And when we obtain any blessing from God, it is by obedience to that law upon which it is predicated." (D&C 130:20–21.)

In very plain terms the Savior has told us, "Of him unto whom much is given much is required; and he who sins against the greater light shall receive the greater condemnation. . . . I, the Lord, am bound when ye do what I say; but when ye do not what I say, ye have no promise." (D&C 82:3, 10.)

6

Infinite Needs and
Finite Resources

In Chapter 2, we discussed our responsibilities as individuals to help with the casualties arising from disasters and the natural consequences of sin in the last days — to reach out beyond the walls of our own church. Some might question why I would choose caring for the needy as an important area of emphasis. We sometimes think in a casual way of caring for others as something we do from time to time to get nice warm fuzzies. In reality, however, the Lord places this responsibility high on his list of priorities.

According to King Benjamin, caring for the needy is necessary in order to receive forgiveness of our transgressions: "And now, for the sake of . . . retaining a remission of your sins from day to day, that ye may walk guiltless before God — I would that ye should impart of your substance to the poor, every man according to that which he hath, such as feeding the hungry, clothing the naked, visiting the sick and administering to their relief, both spiritually and temporally, according to their wants." (Mosiah 4:26.) Since we all need forgiveness, compliance with the Lord's commandment on this issue is an absolute must.

Elder Marion D. Hanks expressed my feelings in his unique and effective style in a general conference address entitled "The Royal Law." After quoting the Savior, who said, "I have set an example for you. . . . I am the light which ye shall hold up — that which ye have seen me do" (3 Nephi 18:16, 24), Elder Hanks commented:

> What [the Savior] did, as we read in a splendid verse in the book of Matthew, was to go "about all Galilee, teaching . . . and preaching the gospel of the kingdom, and healing all manner of . . . disease." (Matt. 4:23.) Matthew also recorded that, as he approached the final events of his earthly ministry, Jesus taught his followers the parable of the sheep and the goats, representing the judgment to come, in which he clearly identified those who will inherit "life eternal" and those who will "go away into everlasting punishment." (Matt. 25:46.) The key difference was that those who should inherit the kingdom with him had developed the habit of helping, had experienced the joy of giving, and the satisfaction of serving — they had responded to the needs of the hungry, thirsty, homeless, the naked, the sick, and those in prison. Well known are his words, the words of comfort to them: "Inasmuch as ye have done it unto one of the least of these my brethren, ye have done it unto me" (Matt. 25:40), while to those who were condemned to "everlasting punishment" he made the sad pronouncement, "Inasmuch as ye did it *not* to one of the least of these, ye did it not to me" (Matt. 25:45; italics added).

Nothing would seem more clear than the high premium the Savior put upon selfless service to others as an indispensable element of Christian conduct and of salvation. Helping, giving, sacrificing are, or should be, as natural as growing and breathing. (*Ensign,* May 1992, p. 9.)

Elder Hanks then quoted the following statement, which President J. Reuben Clark had made in a general conference talk in 1937: "When the Savior came upon the earth he had two great missions; one was to work out the Messiahship, the atonement for the fall, and the fulfillment of the law; the other was the work which he did among his brethren and sisters in the flesh by way of relieving their sufferings. . . . He left as a heritage to those who should come after him in his Church the carrying on of those two great things—work for the relief of the ills and the sufferings of humanity, and the teaching of the spiritual truths which should bring us back into the presence of our Heavenly Father." (Conference Report, April 1937, p. 22.)

Today's headlines are filled with accounts of natural disasters, extreme poverty, wars, terrorism, vicious murders, diseases, and all manner of evil. Some of the greatest disasters are social and are occurring in places of relative peace and prosperity. It is sobering and saddening to view a world so full of pain. It is ironic that at a time when the fullness of the truth is available, society in general is choosing its own way of life under the banner of liberation and freedom. The cause and effect of following incorrect principles is coming into play, and we find pain and suffering everywhere in the form of broken homes, bodies, minds, and spirits.

We live in a world where there are infinite needs for

remedial help, requiring financial and human resources of which there are finite supplies. If we lived in a world where gospel principles were understood and practiced by all mankind, resources would be adequate for all needs. The Lord has assured us, "It is my purpose to provide for my saints, for all things are mine. But it must needs be done in mine own way; and behold this is the way that I, the Lord, have decreed to provide for my saints, that the poor shall be exalted, in that the rich are made low. For the earth is full, and there is enough and to spare." (D&C 104:15–17.)

Unfortunately, gospel principles are not practiced by all mankind; and consequently, a host of problems have arisen and the needs of a failing society appear infinite. In addition, those who have an abundance seem unwilling to "be made low" — to share — and as a result, our resources to help are finite. We know that the world collectively will not repent and live gospel principles; thus, the last days will be filled with much pain and suffering. What is our individual responsibility to help with this infinite need?

The scriptural charges relative to taking care of the casualties of our society are abundantly clear in our dispensation. On January 2, 1831, only nine months after the Church was organized, the Lord said: "For your salvation I give unto you a commandment, for I have heard your prayers, and the poor have complained before me, and the rich have I made, and all flesh is mine, and I am no respecter of persons." (D&C 38:16.) Just one month later the Lord said, "If thou lovest me thou shalt serve me and keep all my commandments. And behold, thou wilt remember the poor, and consecrate of thy properties for their support." (D&C 42:29–30.) Within days, he referred in revelation to this subject again: "Behold, I say unto you, that ye must visit the poor and the needy and administer to their relief." (D&C 44:6.) Apparently the members of the Church hadn't moved fast enough.

The importance of this commandment was dramatically illustrated once again, in June of the same year, in a revelation in which twenty-eight missionaries were called to travel two by two from Kirtland to Jackson County, Missouri, preaching the gospel as they went, and baptizing and conferring the Holy Ghost on those who were converted. Though those who were called to this service were nearly destitute, the Lord told them: "Remember in all things the poor and the needy, the sick and the afflicted, for he that doeth not these things, the same is not my disciple." (D&C 52:40.)

Too often in our day, we think that taking care of the poor is a financial law. As I speak about this subject, however, I refer to much more than what money can buy. I refer to the broad array of afflictions the people in the world are experiencing. People could give every excess dime beyond what is sufficient for their needs and yet fall far short of meeting the needs of the needy. The full meaning of taking care of the poor includes providing support and comfort for those suffering in mind, body, and spirit. Money cannot buy the pure love of Christ. It can only be bought by sacrifice.

It is worthy to note to whom the commandments to take care of the poor were given. To me, the scriptures on this subject suggest that it is more of an individual responsibility than an institutional one. The Church becomes involved in order to make it easier for the members to accomplish this objective. For example, bishops receive sacred donations from members and, with the mantle of their calling, make judgments as to which members are in need. This does not or should not deprive any of us of the opportunity to help each other one-on-one. However, if it were left up to individuals alone, without some form of organization, there would be inefficiencies. Some people would receive more than they need, and others would receive nothing because their need may not be apparent.

In the Lord's wisdom, each bishop is called from among the people over whom he will preside. The bishop knows the people of his ward individually and collectively. He understands the local culture. When he is ordained a bishop, he receives a mantle that enables him to discern to whom help should be given. He has the mandate to seek after the poor and the needy and to call upon the collective resources of his ward. Priesthood quorums and Relief Societies also have opportunities to provide help where organized projects are more efficient than individual projects, and to ascertain needs of individual families through home teaching and visiting teaching.

By contributing tithes and fast offerings, we help people in our ward, stake, nation, and throughout the world. We need the Church organization to help us reach our brothers and sisters in poverty-stricken areas and far-away places. Hence, in taking care of our poor members throughout the world, the Church, as an institution, facilitates our individual responsibility in caring for the needy.

What is the extent of the Church's responsibility to provide humanitarian aid to nonmembers? What priority should this have relative to other responsibilities the Lord has placed on the Church, such as missionary work, temples, family history, and provision for our own poor? What responsibilities do we as individuals have, since we also have finite financial resources and limited available time?

Brigham Young taught, "Before you preach to a starving man to arise and be baptized, first carry him some bread . . . ; first unlock his prison house and let him go free." (*Journal of Discourses* 10:33.)

Elder Harold B. Lee said, "We are talking about converting the world. . . . We might just as well throw our hats in the air and scream as to hope to convert spiritually [a] . . . family or [a] . . . man or [a] . . . nation whose existence has been reduced to the instincts of animal survival. The welfare program has great significance in the Lord's work. We must take care of their material needs and give them a taste of the kind of salvation that they do not have to die to get before we can lift their thinking to a higher plane. . . . [The Lord] stressed the importance of material aid to needy people [in every dispensation] in order that they could be taught the higher spiritual things of life." (Talk given at welfare session of general conference, April 4, 1959; unpublished manuscript.)

Joseph Smith said that in order for us to qualify as good members of the Church, we are required to "feed the hungry, to clothe the naked, to provide for the widow, to dry up the tear of the orphan, to comfort the afflicted, whether in this church, or in any other, or in no church at all," wherever we find them. (*Times and Seasons*, March 15, 1842, p. 732.)

As a scriptural mandate, I like Alma 1:30: "And thus, in their prosperous circumstances, they did not send away any who were naked, or that were hungry, or that were athirst, or that were sick, or that had not been nourished; and they did not set their hearts upon riches; therefore they were liberal to all, both old and young, both bond and free, both male and female, whether out of the church or in the church, having no respect to persons as to those who stood in need."

My testimony on the issue of reaching out beyond the walls of our own church increased several years ago when I was the managing director of the Welfare Services Department of the Church. At that time, we began seeing television documentaries on drought conditions in Ethiopia, with images of mothers holding starving children racked with hunger and disease. This touched the hearts of the world, and we saw an outpouring of compassion that may be unprecedented in its depth and breadth.

Many Latter-day Saints wrote letters to Church headquarters, asking if there were a way the Church could get involved. With sensitivity to the plight of the starving people in Africa and sensitivity to Church members' desires to help, the First Presidency called a special fast in January and again in November 1985. As a result, $11 million was donated to help alleviate the suffering, and a detailed study was made and recommendations were given as to how we could ensure that the contributions reached those in need.

In final preparation to determine how to spend the funds donated in the first special fast, Elder M. Russell Ballard and I went to Ethiopia to see the situation firsthand. There we had some heart-wrenching, soul-stretching, and faith-promoting experiences. Neither of us will be the same again. Some of my most vivid memories are not of the terrible suffering we witnessed, but of the great outpouring of love and service exhibited by nations of the world.

We saw doctors and nurses giving humanitarian service in deplorable settings. They were exhausted but smiling.

We learned of a Catholic priest who had been laboring in the drought in the war-stricken province of Tigray for eleven years. He saw a need and was trying to help long before the television and news accounts made it fashionable.

We saw an elderly Ethiopian man, who was obviously starving to death, stumble into the feeding station camp. On the way to the feeding station, he had passed a deserted village and heard the cry of a baby. Though death was all around him, he searched until he found the baby sitting on the ground next to his dead mother. Despite his own emaciated condition, this man picked up the baby and carried him in his arms for twenty-five miles to the feeding station. His first words were not "I'm hungry" or "Help me." They were "What can be done for this baby I found?"

As Elder Ballard and I walked among thousands of dingy, beaten, and diseased people who were waiting to get into the camp, they would bring their children to us and point to skin sores and ask for ointments. They thought we were doctors. Children would come running after us yelling, "Doctor! Doctor!" Others would call, "Sister! Sister!" What did that mean? The only other white people they had ever seen were doctors and Catholic nuns, so sister did not designate a gender, but a white person who was trying to help. Once after some children called, "Sister! Sister!," Elder Ballard and I looked at each other with the same deep question on our minds. What should we be doing to ensure that "Elder! Elder!" is added to "Doctor! Doctor!" and "Sister! Sister!"?

I believe that we, as members of the Church, should be doing all we can to alleviate suffering and thereby placing "Elder! Elder!" in the vocabulary of those who are in desperate need. At the same time, I envision that title to mean so much more than someone who brings bread. Man cannot live by bread alone. (See Matthew 4:4.) In the eternal scheme of things, the spiritual food we have to offer is of the greatest importance. Any organization or individual can supply food for the body. We have food for the soul. Nevertheless, the body must be reasonably healthy before things of the soul can be fully assimilated.

In Guatemala, an experience with some welfare missionaries had a great impact on me. When the sister missionaries walked onto the meetinghouse grounds, the atmosphere became electric, as people ran and embraced them. I was told the sisters had helped these people through a recent epidemic. They had helped deliver some babies and were present when some members had died. They had brought food for both the soul and the body.

I am thrilled that our full-time missionaries now devote several hours of their week to community service. When followed properly, this program enhances rather than detracts from the primary goal of missionary work. "Elder! Elder!" and "Sister! Sister!" become even more endearing than before because our missionaries are helping with temporal and spiritual salvation.

Knowing that we have been commanded to care for the poor and needy within and without the Church, what priorities should be placed on those two activities?

Joseph F. Smith addressed this when he said, "We feel

that it is the first duty of Latter-day Saints to take care of themselves and of their poor; and then, if we can extend it to others, and as wide and as far as we can extend charity and assistance to others that are not members of the Church, we feel that it is our duty to do it. But first look after the members of our own household. The man who will not provide for his own house, as one of old has said, is worse than an infidel." (*Gospel Doctrine*, p. 308.)

Some have criticized this doctrine. I have heard comments such as, "The Church takes care of its own, but it doesn't do anything for anyone else." This is not only unfair to say, but it is also untrue. However, our first responsibility, our covenant responsibility, is to take care of our own.

To use an extreme analogy, imagine a father of eight children leaving his family destitute while he goes to join the Peace Corps. It won't matter how much good he does in this secondary humanitarian activity; he has failed in life if he abandons his primary responsibility. In a similar vein, it is possible for individuals to get so caught up in humanitarianism that they leave eight million Church members for what they consider a "higher calling." Some may even turn down callings from Church leaders because of their involvement in a "greater cause."

I firmly believe that in today's environment there is room for both caring for our own and helping with the problems in the world's society. Building the kingdom and improving the world are not mutually exclusive. In fact, they are compatible and complementary. When asked which of all the commandments was the greatest, the Lord said, "Thou shalt love the Lord thy God with all thy heart, and with all thy soul, and with all thy mind. This is the first and great commandment. And the second is like unto it, Thou shalt love thy neighbour as thyself." (Matthew 22:37–39.)

The greatest commandment, to love God, was not given priority at the expense or exclusion of the second commandment, to love our neighbor. I cannot comprehend, and indeed, do not feel, that it is possible to love the Lord and not love our neighbors. I have seen persons express tearful testimony and love for the Savior and yet show no warmth whatsoever to God's children. I do not think a sincere love of the Savior is possible without a sincere love of mankind. Neither do I believe it is possible to have sincere love and concern for Church members to the exclusion of the rest of God's children.

Compassion knows no political or religious boundaries. We simply must keep these things in balance as a church and as individuals. Just as there must be balance in missionary work, temple work, and ward work, so we must use wisdom in finding an appropriate balance of financial and human resources in providing for the poor and needy. We, as members of the Church, are outnumbered in the world 665 to 1. We cannot do everything, but still we must do everything we can. If we are thoughtful and prayerful, living one part of the gospel will not be at the expense of another but will be complementary to it.

Today we have the privilege of contributing to the humanitarian fund of the Church. This fund is used in the same manner as the special fast fund was during the Ethiopian crisis. It is a practical accommodation to the members who want to contribute to the plight of those suffering throughout the world irrespective of their religious affiliation. Obviously, individual members cannot, as a general rule, run all over the world responding personally to every disaster or social need. Also, some projects are carried out better on a community basis as opposed to an individual basis. Therefore, the Church has set up a way in which members can participate collectively. We are trying to specialize and become experts in a few things rather than dabble ineffectively in many things.

For example, our Deseret Industries program provides clothing to impoverished countries to be distributed by the Church and other reputable organizations. To give an idea of the magnitude of this effort, we are currently sending out one semitrailer truck full of clothing, firmly packed, each working day of the year. It is quite possible to see a Liberian child in a refugee camp in Ghana wearing a BYU T-shirt. In addition to the clothing distributed, the Church has undertaken over three hundred projects in approximately forty countries in the past eight years. These projects have included emergency responses in areas where disasters have occurred, as well as some long-term development projects, ranging from wells and dams to literacy and polio vaccines.

I cannot emphasize enough that participation in this humanitarian thrust is not meant to be something imposed on members of the Church, but merely made available to them. Neither should it be thought of as the only outlet. There are many good organizations that do wonderful work. We don't want our effort to be viewed as lack of support for any of these organizations. We applaud all organizations that are sincerely trying to improve the lives of God's children.

There is an eternal significance to why the Church is just the facilitator for members in matters of providing for the poor and needy. Two basic goals are met when we fulfill the commandment to care for the poor. The most obvious is to relieve the suffering or lift the spirits of those to whom the service is given. The second is more subtle but is of eternal consequence. It has to do with the sanctification of the giver.

President Marion G. Romney said, "Living the law of consecration exalts the poor and humbles the rich. In the process, both are sanctified. The poor, released from the bondage and humiliating limitations of poverty, are enabled as free men to rise to their full potential, both temporally and spiritually. The rich, by consecration and the imparting of their surplus for the benefit of the poor, not by constraint, but willingly as an act of free will, evidence that charity for their fellowmen characterized by Mormon as 'the pure love of Christ.' (Moro. 7:47.) This will bring both the giver and receiver to the common ground on which the Spirit of God can meet them." (*Ensign,* November 1981, p. 93.)

I have thought of this often and am convinced those who have are actually dependent upon those who have not. Something spiritual happens to individuals when they reach out to help others. President Kimball declared that "as givers gain control of their desires and properly see other needs in light of their own wants, then the powers of the gospel are released in their lives. They learn that by living the great law of consecration they insure not only temporal salvation but also spiritual sanctification." (Conference Report, October 1977, p. 123.)

"It would be a simple thing for the Lord to reveal to [the prophet] where the deposits of oil and precious ores are," President Romney explained. "We could then hire someone to dig them out and we could float in wealth—and we would float in wealth right down to Hades. No, the Lord doesn't really need us to take care of the poor, but *we* need this experience; for it is only through our learning how to take care of each other that we develop within us the Christlike love and disposition necessary to qualify us to return to his presence." (*Ensign,* November 1981, p. 92.)

If individuals completely abdicate to the Church their responsibility of caring for the poor, this beautiful phenomenon does not occur. This is true whether the help goes to members or nonmembers. I say this because there may be a tendency for one to pay tithing and fast offerings and make an occasional donation to the humanitarian fund and then feel that all has been taken care of. The greatest sanctification takes place with person-to-person help. Hence, the greatest compassionate service each of us can give may be in our own neighborhoods and communities. Wherever we live in the world, there is pain and sorrow all around us. We need to take more initiative as individuals in deciding how we can best be of service.

I was pleased with the local projects the Relief Societies throughout the world participated in as part of their sesquicentennial celebration in 1992. Though some thought was given to having wards in more affluent countries reach out across the ocean and help sister wards in impoverished nations, an inspired determination was made that projects would be done on a local basis. I see two great benefits arising from that decision. Both support the doctrine of sanctification resulting from person-to-person service. If projects had been undertaken five thousand miles away instead of in our own backyards, sisters would have missed seeing firsthand the joy in the face of a lonely elderly person in a nursing home, the thanksgiving expressed by a woman in a crisis center, or the tears of gratitude expressed by the invalid whose home was thoroughly cleaned for the first time in years. We don't do these things for immediate credit or the profuse gratitude of those whom we have served, but something very spiritual happens between giver and receiver of personal service. Both are edified and a spiritual bonding takes place. A love comes into the heart that is large enough to encompass not just the person served, but all of God's children.

Another benefit I have seen from having Relief Society sisters involved in projects close to home rather than in distant lands is what my wife and I observed at the sesquicentennial celebration in Ghana. She attended a ward Relief Society meeting where she experienced the sisters' excitement at being involved in a service project. If sisters in the United States had had a project to give something to Ghanaians, the recipients in that country would have appreciated it and loved their American sisters for it, but something would have been lost in the process. They would have met together in a spirit of thanksgiving for what they had received, but they would not have experienced the sanctification of giving. With the program adopted by the general Relief Society presidency, sisters throughout the world were brought together in a common bond of giving. Ghanaians gained much more spirituality by giving with all sisters in the Church than if they had been only the recipients.

All people need to give. This is true of both affluent saints and the poorest of the poor. Poverty is a relative term. It means something much different in one country than in another. There is no common solution or program for every situation. However, principles are universal. We cannot bring everyone to the same economic level. To do so would violate principles and foster dependence rather than independence. People living in each country have the primary responsibility for solving their own problems. They must sacrifice for each other so that they may experience the sanctification that comes from giving.

During a trip to South America a few years ago, I spoke with a stake president whose stake had experienced over 50 percent unemployment during the previous three years. I knew the stake had received less than two hundred dollars from the area office during that period. I asked him how the members had been able to survive without a large infusion of outside help. His answer was that families had helped each other—not just father, mother, sons, and daughters, but uncles, aunts, and cousins. When a cousin got a job, the money earned went to benefit everyone. In addition, ward members looked after each other and shared what they had, however meager. With tears in his eyes, he explained how close his stake members were to each other and to the Lord. Their spirituality had increased manyfold. We could have poured money into this stake from Church headquarters and felt good about it. However, in so doing we would have robbed the members of the opportunity to serve each other and become sanctified in the process.

As I travel in countries where the rate of poverty is high, I am constantly asked "When is the Church going to . . . " questions, such as "When is the Church going to build us a hospital [school, factory, and so forth]?" The solutions to poverty are extremely complex, and the balance between too much aid and not enough is elusive. Our compassion can lead to failure if we give aid without creating independence and self-reliance in the recipient.

However, there is a level of human misery below which no individual should descend as long as others are living in abundance. Can some of us be content living affluent life-styles while others cannot afford the chlorine to purify their water? I struggle constantly with this balance. I believe I have learned a divine truth, however. I cannot become sanctified without serving others, and I will be held accountable if I rob another of the opportunity to give service.

President Romney said, "We are all self-reliant in some areas and dependent in others. Therefore, each of us should strive to help others in areas where we have strengths. At the same time, pride should not prevent us from graciously accepting the helping hand of another when we have a real need. To do so denies another person the opportunity to participate in a sanctifying experience." (*Ensign*, November 1982, p. 93.)

We rob others of the opportunity to serve if we decline their offer of help when we need it. The Church robs its members of the opportunity to serve if we move in too fast with too much every time an emergency arises. If we do this over an extended period of time, members wait for help from headquarters without pitching in and doing all they can for each other first.

None of us can ignore the needs of those around us and have the Spirit of the Lord accompany us. The Savior's example of what we should be doing with our lives is vivid. This is taught by his actions louder than his words. I am increasingly touched by what he did on his way to deliver the Sermon on the Mount as well as by what he said in the sermon.

We should keep the Savior's example in mind as we work together in the Church programs to take care of the poor. If we aren't careful, we can depersonalize an activity by giving money and walking away and assuming "the Church" will do the rest. As individuals, we cannot be spectators to the pain and suffering around us and sit idly by, and then expect sanctification to take place in our lives. We cannot allow organizational lines to build a wall between a person in pain and ourselves, if we are in a position to help. There is a limit to how much we should rely on institutional welfare. To rely too heavily on it would deny us a sanctifying experience.

Moses learned the hard way that he could not administer or minister to every individual in the church by himself. Even if he could have done so, it would not have been right because he would have robbed others of this sanctifying experience. (See Exodus 18:13–26.) The reason he had to delegate to others is obvious. However, without the proper perspective, there is danger in setting up an organizational structure to provide for more efficiency.

This danger is true today with the establishment of the welfare program and humanitarian service effort if members do not understand principles. This efficient organization, which takes care of the poor, provides a convenient sense of security that we, as individuals, have done all that we can. It can provide an organizational wall between us and people in need. At the first sign that someone is in need, we automatically release ourselves from reaching out because, after all, we are not that person's bishop, or home teacher, or visiting teacher. Often there is a cry for help that has our name preceding it, and you or I may be the only one who can hear the cry. I have heard some of those cries and cannot always delegate the comforting to someone else without being held accountable. Much discernment is needed to identify those times so that the order of the Church is not violated.

But even though Moses set up a system whereby it became possible to nurture the children of Israel, I would be very surprised if he stopped helping individuals with what available time he did have. The Savior himself did not delegate all compassionate service to his disciples, but spent his life doing all he could to help the one. Therefore, I assume we must all go and do likewise.

I trust that we will continue to see humanitarian aid given by the Church as long as it effectively facilitates our individual desires to reach out to the poor and needy. Bishops will continue to be the key figures in coordinating our responsibility to take care of our own. However, the primary responsibility for the care of the poor falls on us as individuals. We should give financial contributions when possible, but this alone is not complete. We must also give of ourselves. We can ofttimes give of ourselves when a financial contribution is not possible.

We constantly hear pleas for more missionary work, more family history, more meaningful time with our families, and so forth. The purpose of this book is to call for a spiritual revival which, in effect, asks for more of many things. Speaking as a father, I must admit that on many days the needs of my six children are so great that I don't have the time or energy to look beyond the walls of our own home. If I magnify my feelings many times, I can understand how my wife feels. I must also confess I have been guilty on some occasions of being so weighed down with the problems of the world when I get home that I have failed my children during their time of need. It's an extremely difficult balance. But with everything I have written, I want you to know that our greatest responsibility is in our own immediate and extended family. Sanctification comes from service rendered to our own families as well as to strangers.

I realize that for some, with the demands placed on them by their families, close friends, and Church callings, there is not much left with which to save the world. It is not my objective to take anyone on a guilt trip, but rather to teach some principles of caring for the needy. Only the individual can know his or her own unique situation and can determine how these principles can be applied in each particular circumstance.

My promise is that as you review these infinite needs in relation to your own finite resources, you will be able to formulate a plan that will provide the appropriate balance. I also promise you that the things the gospel asks of us are not mutually exclusive, but are complementary to each other.

I know that increased spirituality is a natural consequence of reaching out to others. As we do so, we feel closer to the Lord and begin to understand why he spent so much of his time blessing the lives of the poor and needy. And as we do as he did, spiritual revival will take place in our lives.

7

Our Commitment
to Morality

No transgression on earth or within the Church takes a bigger toll on spirituality and causes more devastation in the lives of people than immorality. We are constantly bombarded with what is sometimes called a new morality, which is nothing more than the same old immorality. Things that would have made us all blush just a few years ago are so commonly heard and seen today that it is difficult not to become desensitized.

We are all grateful that some "vices," such as smoking, are becoming no longer acceptable for the majority of society. Unfortunately, a much larger transgression, the one next to murder in its seriousness, seems to be more accepted than ever. I am speaking, of course, of premarital and extramarital sexual relations.

Our society, and those in it who control the mass media

in particular, seems to have a preoccupation with this subject. It is blinding them and some of us to those things which are "virtuous, lovely, or of good report or praiseworthy." (Article of Faith 13.)

I long for the day when, in the entertainment world, all of the four-letter words will be used up and so worn out that we can at least return to one three-letter word — *wit*. It would probably be too much to dream of having all objectionable four-letter words, including *gore* and *lust*, purged, and the seven-, eight-, and nine-letter words of *romance, suspense,* and *adventure* reintroduced.

Elder Boyd K. Packer spoke of the deterioration of morality in the world in a general conference talk in April 1992:

> Today I speak to members of the Church as an environmentalist. My message is not on the *physical* but on the *moral and spiritual* environment in which we must raise our families. As we test the *moral* environment, we find the *pollution* index is spiraling upward.
>
> The Book of Mormon depicts humanity struggling through a "mist of darkness" and defines the darkness as the "temptations of the devil." (1 Ne. 8:23; 12:17.) So dense was that *moral pollution* that many followed "strange roads" and "fell away into forbidden paths and were lost." (See 1 Ne. 8:23–32.)
>
> The deliberate pollution of the fountain of life now clouds our moral environment. The gift of mortal life and the capacity to kindle other lives is a supernal blessing. Its worth is *incalculable!*
>
> The rapid, sweeping deterioration of values is characterized by a preoccupation — even an obsession — with the procreative act. Abstinence before marriage and fidelity within it are openly scoffed at — marriage and parenthood ridiculed as burdensome, unnecessary. Mod-

esty, a virtue of a refined individual or society, is all but gone.

The adversary is jealous toward all who have the power to beget life. He cannot beget life; he is impotent. He and those who followed him were cast out and forfeited the right to a mortal body. His angels even begged to inhabit the bodies of swine. (See Matt. 8:31.) And the revelations tell us that "he seeketh that all men might be miserable like unto himself." (2 Nephi 2:27.)

With ever fewer exceptions, what we see and read and hear have the mating act as a central theme. Censorship is forced offstage as a violation of individual freedom. That which should be absolutely private is disrobed and acted out center stage. In the shadows backstage are addiction, pornography, perversion, infidelity, abortion, and—saddest of them all—incest and molestation. In company with them now is a plague of biblical proportion. And all of them are on the increase. . . .

While we pass laws to reduce pollution of the earth, any proposal to protect the moral and spiritual environment is shouted down and marched against as infringing upon liberty, agency, freedom, the right to choose. Interesting how one virtue, when given exaggerated or fanatical emphasis, can be used to batter down another, with freedom, a virtue, invoked to protect *vice*. Those determined to transgress see any regulation of their lifestyle as interfering with their agency and seek to have their actions condoned by making them legal. . . .

The source of life is now relegated to the level of unwed pleasure, bought and sold and even defiled in satanic rituals. Children of God can willfully surrender to their carnal nature and, without remorse, defy the laws of morality and degrade themselves even below the beasts. (*Ensign,* May 1992, 66–68.)

Elder David B. Haight put it this way: "Thoughtful, concerned people in many areas and nations of the world, as well as Latter-day Saints, are concerned with the growing pressures and influence of a disturbing cultural movement downgrading social and religious values and standards of morality. Each succeeding generation has weakened or lessened previous Christ-centered ideals and values. . . . The actual signs of the times are threatening. Where will they lead? I, for one, am concerned. Previous periods of moral decline brought forth divine attention. In past times, as at present, prophets of God have delivered a voice of warning. The Lord said to Ezekiel, 'I have made thee a watchman unto the house of Israel: therefore hear the word . . . , and give them warning from me.' (Ezek. 3:17.) From what we are witnessing happening in the world around us, I am impressed today to raise a voice of warning for mankind to prepare—by repentance—for the great day of the Lord. (See D&C 1:11–12.)" (*Ensign*, November 1992, p. 74.)

The *Salt Lake Tribune* on August 25, 1992, published an article entitled "American Families Unlikely to Return to 1950s Model." Reading this article, one almost gets the opinion that the author is speaking of the emancipation of families as opposed to the slavery to which many have submitted. Two natural consequences of moral transgression are broken homes and children born out of wedlock. With these sins in mind, I submit portions of the article as a case in point of how people have come to accept the consequences:

> A half-century of change in family structure is likely to slow in the 1990s, but there is no likelihood America will return to the "Ozzie and Harriet" model of yesteryear, a private study concluded Monday.
> "Valuing the family should not be confused with

valuing a particular family form," said the report by the Population Reference Bureau, which analyzed census and other government data. "Social legislation, or 'pro-family' policies, narrowly designed to reinforce only one model of the American family is likely to be shortsighted and have the unintended consequence of weakening, rather than strengthening, family ties," the report said.

The "Ozzie and Harriet" model of 1950s television fame—a bread-winning husband and a wife who stayed home with the children—once was the dominant pattern in America. Now, one in five married couples with children fits that stereotype, the report said. About 36% of all American families are married couples with children, but a growing number of those are "blended" stepfamilies. One in three Americans is a member of a stepfamily and that is expected to rise to nearly one in two by the turn of the century, the report said.

Much has changed since the start of the Baby Boom after World War II:

• The average age at first marriage is highest in a century—26.3 years for men and 24.1 for women.

• The marriage rate fell 30% between 1970 and 1990, while the divorce rate increased 40%.

• More than half of all mothers with preschool children worked outside the home in 1991, compared with one in five in 1960.

• One in four babies is born to an unmarried mother, compared with one in 20 in 1960.

• Nearly one in eight families was headed by a single parent last year, and that parent was five times more likely to be a woman.

• About a quarter of all children, more than 16 million of them, lived with only one parent in 1991. That is double the percentage of 1970 and nearly three times that of 1960.

It doesn't take much analysis to determine how fidelity

before and during marriage would affect those figures. The victims of this shift are the children who are not growing up in homes that are ideal (what the report calls "Ozzie and Harriet" homes). As these children reach adulthood, the possibility of their history repeating itself or of their following the traditions of their fathers and/or mothers is most likely. One could easily project a geometric increase in problems created by broken homes.

Does it not become obvious as to why immorality is placed next to murder in its seriousness?

I would like to reach out to the youth in particular on this issue, although adults have fallen victim to these insidious sins in droves. To all I say, we will remain much safer and infinitely happier if we will place our energies in current obedience rather than saving them for future repentance.

Why do we speak to the youth so much about living chaste, moral lives? Because they will be happier by so doing. They should be living pure lives now—not just before they go on a mission, just before they are married in the temple, just before the birth of their first child, or just before their death.

Few of us question the necessity of living a pure life prior to dying because we know a judgment day lies ahead. However, life is full of milestones that require a purity of life before desired blessings can accrue to us. Most Latter-day Saints are familiar with the scripture regarding procrastination recorded in Alma 34. Let me paraphrase it for the milestones of mission and marriage:

"For behold, this day is the time for men and women to prepare for missions and temple marriages; behold this day is the day for men and women to perform their labors.

Ye cannot say, when ye enter the Missionary Training Center or kneel at the altar in the temple, that I will repent, that I will return to God. Nay, ye cannot say this; for the same spirit which doth possess your bodies at the time ye go into the MTC or temple, will have power to possess your body in the mission field or in your marriage." (See Alma 34:32, 34.)

The strongest counsel I can give the youth is to stay worthy. Prospective missionaries should make certain they enter the MTC worthily, and that they are honest with their local priesthood leaders if they have given in to temptation.

This is what may happen to those who aren't honest in these matters. The Spirit is so strong at the MTC that their guilt will be intense. They will go and talk to a branch president, and he will send them to a General Authority, if the transgression is grievous and recent. They may then have to return to their local priesthood leaders and tell them that they weren't honest in their interviews, and face their families and friends. To our young people I would plead: Please get rid of your bag of rocks before you enter the MTC. More importantly, *stay clean.*

An attitude developing among many of our youth says, in essence, "Eat, drink, and be merry, for tomorrow I go on my mission." Another false notion is, "It's easier to repent than to resist." Each of us may repent of our mistakes, it is true. However, no one ever has and no one ever will escape the natural consequences of transgression. The Savior's atonement allows us to repent, but repentance is painful and it takes time to heal. If those who are repenting have not felt the pain, they have not fully repented. Prospective missionaries should stay clean so that they can maximize their impact on those waiting to hear the gospel and also minimize their guilt, tears, and regrets.

Some time ago I was asked to interview a young man who had been guilty of a serious moral transgression. I asked his priesthood leader how long it had been since the transgression had occurred, and the response was, "Three weeks."

I just about flew out of my chair. "Are you seriously considering sending this young man on a mission?"

He said, "Well, he's had a horrible childhood, and we've worked very hard with him and his family. He's already received his call, and the farewell is scheduled for next week. He feels horrible about the incident, and I feel that if we can get him into the mission field, the atmosphere will be conducive to his complete repentance and we just might save this boy."

I couldn't believe my ears. I was closer to suggesting that the priesthood leader be released than I was to clearing the young man for a mission. A mission is not a place for missionaries to repent, but for calling sinners to repentance. Missionaries are not being sent on missions to gain a testimony, but to bear their testimonies. The experiences they encounter will increase their testimony, but until they have one and are worthy to have the Spirit with them, their effectiveness is limited.

There is a common feeling among many young people, and unfortunately among too many adults, that the only real discomfort or penalty for serious transgression is the pain and embarrassment attendant with confessing the transgression to their bishop. This is only the beginning. One cannot immediately have the Spirit of the Holy Ghost as a constant companion by simply walking into the bishop's office, confessing a sin, and walking out again. None of us believe in deathbed repentance. Why do so many of us accept "mission bed" repentance? It matters little that a prospective missionary learns his or her discussions well and is the best in the class on the commitment pattern, gaining a person's trust, and all the other techniques, if he or she does not also have the Spirit.

If missionaries are going to kindle a fire of testimony within the breasts of investigators, their own torches must be burning. Impurity douses the fire of one's torch just as surely as if it were dunked into a pool of water.

Why should missionaries keep themselves clean prior to serving a mission? It is as simple as this: "There is a law, irrevocably decreed in heaven before the foundations of this world, upon which all blessings are predicated— And when we obtain any blessing from God, it is by obedience to that law upon which it is predicated." (D&C 130:20–21.)

It goes without saying that there are more reasons for young people keeping themselves morally clean than being able to go on a mission. Another one is to make certain they are able to continue their spiritual growth and keep the lines of revelation open between them and our Father in heaven.

A bishop, stake president, and General Authority may clear someone to go on a mission, but the ultimate peace and reassurance of forgiveness can only come from our Heavenly Father. Priesthood leaders—even General Authorities—can be deceived by prospective missionaries who are not being completely honest (although I wouldn't count on it). However, the Lord and the Spirit of the Holy Ghost cannot be fooled, and the Spirit will not dwell in an unclean tabernacle. I have spoken plainly about being worthy to serve a mission. Now I wish to speak about another aspect of morality, also in plainness in order that it not be misunderstood.

Some of our youth "draw the line" in different places relative to physical relationships, and they have the uncanny ability to rationalize and feel comfortable with where they have drawn the line. The phrases "going all the way," "heavy petting," and "light petting" are commonly used. Let me give you an analogy of what these statements mean to me:

"Going all the way" is like allowing someone to put your feet in cement and dropping you into a pool of water that is over your head. "Heavy petting" is the same, except that the water comes to the top of your nose. You can see, but without some repenting you're going to spiritually drown. With "light petting," the water comes just above the lips. You can breathe in a little air through your nose, but life is miserable and drowning can occur. To carry the analogy one step further, "making out" brings the water level only to your neck, but in the event of a passionate storm, a tidal wave may bring about your spiritual demise. You need to learn the early warning signs of a storm and, more importantly, heed them. "I just got carried away" or "I guess I got in over my head" are lame excuses.

For those who have gotten in over their heads, there is a way back; however, my emphasis here is not on repentance, but on steering clear of anything that will result in the need to repent. I believe the pendulum has swung too far in talking repentance rather than preventing through obedience.

Young people would do well to ask themselves this

question: When I get married, am I going to be faithful to my spouse? It seems incomprehensible to most of us that we would cheat on our spouses, right?

Now they should ask themselves another question: Should I be faithful to my future husband or wife even before I know who he or she is? I'm sure each young person hopes his or her future spouse is being true now and is saving those things reserved for marriage.

In the Doctrine and Covenants we read: "In the celestial glory there are three heavens or degrees; and in order to obtain the highest, a man must enter into this order of the priesthood [meaning the new and everlasting covenant of marriage]; and *if he does not, he cannot obtain it.*" (D&C 131:1–3; italics added.) Why can't he obtain it? Not just because he didn't obey a celestial commandment; rather, it is because he didn't become a celestial being.

We are limited in our spiritual development as long as we are single. There is a spiritual development which can only be obtained when a man and a woman join their incomplete selves into a complete couple through celestial marriage. In order to receive the highest degree of the celestial kingdom, a person must have not only a temple marriage, but also a celestial relationship. As a man and woman grow spiritually, the Holy Ghost celestializes not only their individual spirits, but also their spiritual relationship until they eventually acquire all the attributes necessary to become a god and goddess. There is a certain degree of personal glory one cannot obtain without the spiritual association of male and female in marriage. Infidelity in marriage and prior to marriage can delay, if not cancel, godhood. This is why morality is such an important commandment.

One of my favorite explanations of why this commandment is so important was given by Jeffrey R. Holland
in a talk he delivered to the students at Brigham Young
University. I include here but a short segment:

> Human intimacy, that sacred, physical union or-
> dained of God for a married couple, deals with a symbol
> that demands special sanctity. Such an act of love be-
> tween a man and a woman is — or certainly was ordained
> to be — a symbol of total union: union of their hearts,
> their hopes, their lives, their love, their family, their
> future, their everything. It is a symbol that we try to
> suggest in the temple with a word like *seal*. . . .
>
> But such a total, virtually unbreakable union, such
> an unyielding commitment between a man and a
> woman, can come only with the proximity and perma-
> nence afforded in a marriage covenant, with the union
> of all that they possess — their very hearts and minds,
> all their days and all their dreams. They work together,
> they cry together, they enjoy Brahms and Beethoven
> and breakfast together, they sacrifice and save and live
> together for all the abundance that such a totally intimate
> life provides such a couple. And the external symbol of
> that union, the physical manifestation of what is a far
> deeper spiritual and metaphysical bonding, is the phys-
> ical blending that is part of — indeed, a most beautiful
> and gratifying expression of — that larger, more complete
> union of eternal purpose and promise. . . .
>
> You must wait until you can give everything, and
> you cannot give everything until you are at least legally
> and, for Latter-day Saint purposes, eternally pro-
> nounced as one. To give illicitly that which is not yours
> to give (remember — "you are not your own") and to give
> only part of that which cannot be followed with the gift
> of your whole heart and your whole life and your whole
> self is its own form of emotional Russian roulette. If you

persist in sharing part without the whole, in pursuing satisfaction devoid of symbolism, in giving parts and pieces and inflamed fragments only, you run the terrible risk of such spiritual, psychic damage that you may undermine both your physical intimacy and your wholehearted devotion to a truer, later love. You may come to that moment of real love, of total union, only to discover to your horror that what you should have saved has been spent and that only God's grace can recover that piecemeal dissipation of your virtue.

A good Latter-day Saint friend, Dr. Victor L. Brown, Jr., has written of this issue:

"Fragmentation enables its users to counterfeit intimacy. . . . If we relate to each other in fragments, at best we miss full relationships. At worst, we manipulate and exploit others for our gratification. Sexual fragmentation can be particularly harmful because it gives powerful physiological rewards which, though illusory, can temporarily persuade us to overlook the serious deficits in the overall relationship. Two people may marry for physical gratification and then discover that the illusion of union collapses under the weight of intellectual, social, and spiritual incompatibilities. . . .

"Sexual fragmentation is particularly harmful because it is particularly deceptive. The intense human intimacy that should be enjoyed in and symbolized by sexual union is counterfeited by sensual episodes which suggest—but cannot deliver—acceptance, understanding, and love. Such encounters mistake the end for the means as lonely, desperate people seek a common denominator which will permit the easiest, quickest gratification." (*Human Intimacy: Illusion and Reality* [Salt Lake City: Parliament Publishers, 1981], pp. 5–6.) (*On Earth As It Is in Heaven* [Salt Lake City: Deseret Book, 1989], 189–91.)

One of the traps soon-to-be engaged or engaged couples fall into is this: "Well, after all, we are going to be married anyway, so it's not as serious as if we were just dating." This is dangerous because, first, the sides of the roads are cluttered with fallen men and women who lost their virtue to someone they thought they would be marrying anyway, and second, until marriage, certain things are forbidden.

Another dangerous, if not lethal, line is drawn by some married persons. They rationalize inappropriate emotional relationships with individuals other than their spouses by saying, "We didn't engage in anything physical." How ridiculous to think that the Spirit will celestialize a marriage relationship and the individuals within that relationship when they are not being true to each other emotionally and spiritually, even if they do not break the physical law of chastity!

Can anything impede spiritual growth more for a single person or be more damaging to a celestial relationship after marriage than immorality? Inappropriate relationships violate more than a physical law. Immorality violates an emotional and spiritual relationship with a spouse, whether committed prior to or subsequent to marriage. It also violates a relationship with God, thereby clogging the channel of revelation. Immorality sets up a barrier that cannot be penetrated by the Holy Ghost.

The most sacred relationship in life—husband and wife, priest and priestess, god and goddess—should be built on a solid foundation. This is why purity and fidelity both before and during marriage is so important. We need a revival in our commitment to morality.

8

Being Worthy
of Temple Blessings

The last "commandment" I have chosen to address is that of receiving and staying worthy of our temple blessings. As a general rule, we don't think of this as a commandment, but as a reward for keeping our covenants. Obviously, if we are worthy to go to the temple, we are being obedient to many of the Lord's commandments. Still, many who are living true to most of the requirements of receiving their temple blessings let relatively small things stand in the way of receiving infinite rewards.

Living a temple-worthy life culminates in receiving the blessings, but one must still participate in temple ordinances prior to being able to receive the blessings therefrom. Failing to do so is akin to failing to be baptized, as many investigators of the Church do, even after having received a testimony.

I can't comprehend how insecure I would feel traveling throughout these last days without the full armor available through temple blessings. While many of those blessings lie in the future, what we receive in our lives today justifies whatever small sacrifice it would take to become temple worthy.

I have in my possession a pocketknife that belonged to my grandfather. It has little monetary value, but it is priceless as far as I am concerned. My grandfather died when I was fourteen years of age. I still remember him standing over the rotating stone wheel he used to sharpen the knife. The blade is probably two-thirds its original size, partly due to use but mostly because of the frequent sharpening.

I spent the summers of my childhood with my grandparents on their farm in Hoytsville, Utah. It was difficult the first summer after he died. On my first day at the house that summer, Grandma handed me the pocketknife and said, "Pa would have wanted you to have this."

Whenever I look at the knife, I have a flood of memories of Grandpa's farm. Those were golden months of my childhood. Things were much less complex on a farm in Utah in 1950.

My most vivid and profound memory is of something that happened approximately a year before my grandfather's death. I was thirteen years old and we were sitting in the living room having a grandfather/grandson talk. He said, "Let me show you a picture of the happiest day of my life."

He went over to the wall and took down a picture and handed it to me. The photograph was of Grandma and Grandpa and their eleven children and their spouses standing in front of the east doors of the Salt Lake Temple. He told me the story. It was his seventy-eighth birthday and he and Grandma and all of their children, together with their spouses, had attended a temple session. A photographer from the *Church News* thought it was a unique situation and took the picture of their temple party.

"Your grandma and I have been married fifty-three years and all of our children are accounted for," Grandpa told me. He shed tears and I shed tears, even though I had little comprehension about what he was feeling. All I knew was that he was touched with joy and love for his family. It has been about forty years since that trip to the temple, and all of their children are still accounted for, although many have passed through the veil.

A few years ago, one of my fifty-one cousins asked me to perform his sealing to his wife and son. While I was in the temple contemplating what I might say to make the ceremony as spiritual as it ought to be, I once again thought of my grandparents, and this impression came to me: "Remember the afternoon when I told you about the happiest day of my life? We had all of our children with us. Glenn, how are your cousins doing and what are you doing about it?"

I realized from that experience that those who have passed on continue to be vitally concerned about their posterity. No matter what assignments are given to us in the hereafter, they take second place to our primary responsibility.

The question about my cousins haunted me for over a year. I felt a responsibility, but I did not know what to do about it. Finally I had an idea and acted upon it. I located the addresses of my fifty-one cousins and sent them each the following letter:

I am sending this letter to each of the fifty-one Pace cousins. It is prompted by feelings I have had over the last couple of years, which came to a head as I prepared some comments for Uncle Vernal's funeral. There was something about losing the youngest of our uncles that caused some serious reflection on my life and our great family heritage. I had an outpouring of love and appreciation for Grandma and Grandpa Pace and longed to visit with them once more. I had similar feelings about our uncles and aunt who have passed on to the other side. I also had fond memories of each of you, my cousins.

Last year I was in Nauvoo and was taken to three sites that had been owned by our great-great-grandparents, Eliza and Elisha Pace. They joined the Saints in Nauvoo in 1839. On his birthday in October of 1844, Elisha died. In 1846 our widowed great-great-grandmother left Nauvoo for Nebraska, and in 1848 she made her trek to Utah with her children: Edwin (17), George Milton (12, our great-grandfather), and Amanda (6). As I stood on the ground where they once lived in Nauvoo, thinking of their sacrifice, it was as though Eliza asked me a question: "Have you honored your heritage?" On behalf of Elisha and Eliza, I pass that sobering question to you.

On June 21, 1949, those of us who were alive attended Grandma and Grandpa Pace's fiftieth wedding-anniversary celebration. I was nine years old but vividly remember the family mingling together and savoring the outbursts of that unique Pace laugh. I remember Grandma walking around with Grandpa, her hand on his arm, and visiting with their family. It was a beautiful summer day and we all basked in the warmth of the sun and the love of our family.

In June of 1987, I had the privilege of sealing one of our cousins to his wife and son. In the temple while I was thinking about Grandma and Grandpa, the following question came into my mind: "Remember when I told you about the happiest day of my life? How are your cousins doing and what are you doing about it?" I have thought about that and hence my attempt to do something about it.

I would like to propose a reunion of cousins for Grandma and Grandpa's ninety-second wedding anniversary, June 21, 1991. The reason for setting it that far ahead is twofold: (1) So plans can be made, and (2) to give those who may not have a current temple recommend the time to remedy that situation if they are so inclined. The highlight of our reunion would be for all of us, and our spouses, to go on an endowment session in the Salt Lake Temple and have our picture taken on the east steps of the temple.

Of course, we would also invite our parents. I was tempted to say "parents still living," but I am certain parents from both sides of the veil will attend with Grandma and Grandpa.

I would welcome any comments, suggestions, and help you could give to bring this dream to fruition. To those who may be struggling, please let me know if there is anything I can do to help. I love you all and look forward to this reunion with much joy.

The following excerpt is from my journal of June 21, 1991: "We went to the Salt Lake Temple as part of our cousins reunion. There were 86 cousins, uncles, and aunts out of a total 110 possible. It was a very inspirational experience. I kept feeling that I couldn't quite take it all in, that there was a lot more going on than I was perceiving. The officiators were quite touched by the occasion and I felt they gave an extra beautiful presentation and were fairly emotional in a number of instances. One of them told me that this was a special group because he could feel it. They were all very kind to us.

"One of my favorite parts was going into the celestial room and greeting cousins there and having the feeling that family members from the other side of the veil were also there. We felt extra close at that point. Afterwards, we changed our clothes and met outside by the east doors of the temple, and literally covered all of the steps, and had our picture taken. It will be a perfect memento of this occasion and will be treasured by the cousins and their children for years to come."

The occasion was perfect except for the fact that not all of us were there. We need to keep encouraging our family to make themselves eligible to receive of the fullness. A spiritual revival needs to continue in our family.

At this point in my life I understand much more than I did when I was thirteen why Grandpa called that day the happiest day of his life. This understanding was intensified recently because we saw three of our children married in the temple within four months' time.

The full impact of "losing" half of our family in such a short period hit me during family vacation. We have had a tradition of spending two weeks on the beach in San Diego. Just three days prior to our leaving for California, the first couple married informed us they wouldn't be able to come. This left us with two engaged couples and two teenagers.

With less than half the vacation gone, one of the engaged couples returned home because of work commitments. Then the other couple, Rikki and Ryan, informed us they were going home in two more days to make wedding preparations.

My wife and I decided this would be fine because we could give good, quality time to the two teenagers who would be left. But those plans were shattered as each of them, individually, approached us and asked, "Since this weekend is the 24th of July, can I go back with Rikki and Ryan?" This left us alone for the remaining three days.

In years past we would have loved three days without the children, but at this point in our lives we could feel them slipping through our fingers. I found myself sitting alone on the beach, doing a lot of "remember when-ing." Finally, having felt sorry for myself long enough, I decided it was time to get into the wedding spirit and enjoy the positive side of seeing my children married at the right time, in the right place, to the right persons.

As we went through these experiences, my wife and I felt much joy and rejoicing in our family. I'm going to share some of the inner feelings of my heart. My objective is to provide an incentive to young people to set their goal to be married in the temple and live worthy of it. I would also encourage those married couples who have not yet been to the temple to work toward that goal.

I was blessed with the privilege of performing the three marriages and wondered how I could do justice to the occasions. I spent some time in the temple to seek the proper spirit and offered a prayer that I might say those things that would make the events as sacred and special as the couples deserved. Even as those words left my lips, however, I got the impression that no words in any language in the world can do justice to the importance of a temple marriage.

I have become convinced that we are completely dependent on the Spirit to convey the deep import and beauty of the moment. On such occasions we need to be spiritually sensitive to what we feel, and not limit the communication to what is said. These are golden moments that should be savored. My feelings are described beautifully in a phrase from the hymn "How Great Thou Art": "I scarce can take it in." (*Hymns,* no. 86.)

The three marriages took place in the Salt Lake Temple. This temple, like all others, is a hallowed place, a house of the Lord. He visits his house through his spirit and in person. We have accounts of this fact. In addition, the Lord's anointed apostles and prophets meet in that holy house every week to discuss the challenges and opportunities facing the kingdom and to seek, in all sincerity of heart, guidance from the Lord.

To witness the sacred event that would be taking place in this house of the Lord, each of the couples invited those persons who meant the most to them in their lives — close family members and intimate friends. Many eyes were moist because of the love we had for them and the happiness and joy we felt for them. In addition, we all had a love for and devotion to the Savior, which magnified our love for them. We love them more than they could comprehend at this stage of their lives. Speaking for their parents and grandparents, I can say that we experienced joy and rejoicing in our posterity. Words cannot describe it. We are grateful for the obedient lives they lived that qualified them to be in the holy temple.

There was a spiritual radiance in the face of each bride and groom that was brought about by the righteous lives they have lived, the love they have for the Lord Jesus

Christ, and the love they have for each other. We often hear people express feelings about how beautiful and glowing a bride is. I saw a glow much brighter than that of a new bride. I saw the glow of a worthy, choice, handmaiden of the Lord. In the groom, I saw the glow of a worthy warrior of the Lord.

I have mentioned the holiness of the temple and the love we who were invited to share this sacred event have for the couples. And that is not all. Others who loved them were also permitted to experience the joy of the moment. I am certain there were angels in the room. These angels were not strangers, but rather those who would have been there had the Lord not called them home earlier. They are busy in the work of the Lord, but in the spirit world and throughout all eternity, the family continues as the most important work. Death does not release a person from family responsibilities nor from a deep love for families followed by a yearning to be with us whenever possible.

On those unique occasions, as grateful as I was to hold the great sealing power, I was more grateful to hold the title of father and patriarch of our home.

Prior to my daughter's wedding, I had the usual feelings of all fathers of the bride. I was giving my daughter to another man. As I worked through that, I had the following thoughts and insights.

For several years, I said my evening prayers at her bedside. I felt such an innocence and purity in her room that it became my sacred grove. As I would pray, she would run her fingers through my hair. Those were sacred moments.

I always wanted to show my daughter new things I had discovered, and she would point out a beauty or a thought I had missed. She wrote thoughtful notes that would raise my spirits and put my life in the proper perspective. She would sometimes come to me with a surprise behind her back. I never knew whether it would be a handful of wild flowers or a fistful of potato bugs. She found equal beauty in both. I loved to look into her eyes. They are soft, loving, nonjudgmental, curious, understanding, and yes, often mischievous.

With these feelings, I both longed for and dreaded her wedding day. My prayer for her was always that somewhere, sometime, she would meet a worthy young man who would be able to see and love the deeply spiritual things I have admired in her for so long. It is a sad day, but a necessary one, when a father realizes that his daughter cannot progress much further without the introduction of another male. That day came to me not many years ago when I began to observe a void I could not fill. As the years went on, the void got larger. I knew it could only be filled by her husband. No wisdom, humor, or companionship of mine could fill that void. I alone could not take her much higher.

When that realization sets in, the intensity of a father's prayers increases relative to her finding the right man. He prays for someone who will love her for the right reasons. He prays for someone who loves the Lord and lives the commandments. He prays for someone who will provide an adequate living without making his career the most important part of his life. He prays for someone who will be a good father to his children, who will honor his father and mother, who will put his family and church first, and who will be sensitive to the Spirit and able to receive revelation to guide his family.

It occurred to me that the bridegroom's parents had been praying for the same things for their son and his future bride. They had been following the same road map, a map that leads us all back to the common place from which we began our separate journeys: back home to our heavenly parents and our Savior Jesus Christ, who designed the map and paid the price of our travels.

I felt a great love for the mothers who spent their married lives completely and unselfishly benefitting their children. I hold these women up as examples of true womanhood, even that of priestess and goddess in much more than embryo form.

That summer, the three couples each set a goal that placed the Lord in the center of their relationship. The relationship between a couple and the Savior has been described as a triangle, but I would like to suggest it is a circle with the Savior in the center. There are others in the circle who are necessary in our quest for perfection. Parents, brothers, sisters, grandparents, uncles, aunts, cousins, nieces, nephews, and friends—all are an integral part of the circle. We did not go to the temple to see these couples join each other by disconnecting from us, but to join with them in making our connection more complete. Our love for them and theirs for us will be magnified by their marriage, not diminished. Love is infinite in quantity and quality. We are eternally mothers, fathers, sisters, and brothers.

Just as I discovered that I couldn't fill the void in my daughter that is reserved for a husband, so they will discover that their love for each other is incomplete without relatives and friends. Also with this eternal union, they doubled the size of their circle by adding "in-law" to each of the designations of family members. I can testify that they can love their in-laws as much as they love their own families. Love is capable of infinite expansion. I can't even relate to in-law jokes because I love my mother-in-law and father-in-law and my brothers-in-law and sisters-in-law as my own.

In this context, we can see that what takes place in the temple affects much more than two young people in love. It is not a private thing. A popular phrase today is "It's my life." No, it's *our* life. Two people are sealed together. The sealing automatically provides that their children will be born under the covenant, and as part of that blessing, the family will be together forever. They will be with their brothers and sisters, grandparents, uncles, aunts, and cousins forever.

As parents, we ask for no special thanks, but in my heart, the best expression of gratitude will be for our children to "pass it on" to their children. In twenty years or so, we want to be with our children when our grandchildren are married at the altar.

Husbands and wives are mutually dependent on each other for their spiritual development into celestial beings. We know that we cannot enter into the highest degree of the celestial kingdom without entering into the new and everlasting covenant of marriage and being faithful to it. We cannot reach that degree of perfection without an exchange of male and female spirit. We will learn spiritual things from each other that cannot be acquired in any other way. We will perfect a love for all of God's children as we obtain this spiritual love for each other. Teaching us to become gods is the ultimate goal of the gospel. Usually this is put in the context of perfecting the saints.

Joseph Smith put it more plainly: "You have got to learn how to be Gods yourselves, and to be kings and priests to God, the same as all Gods have done before you, namely, by going from one small degree to another, and from a small capacity to a great one; from grace to grace, from exaltation to exaltation, until you attain to the resurrection of the dead, and are able to dwell in everlasting burnings, and to sit in glory, as do those who sit enthroned in everlasting power." (*Teachings of the Prophet Joseph Smith* [Salt Lake City: Deseret Book, 1976], pp. 346–47.)

It is for the purpose of giving this process its full power that I performed the marriage ceremonies for my children and their spouses. This fact gives so much more meaning to the already meaningful purpose of sealing couples together for time and for all eternity. It is one thing to promise them that they will be together for time and all eternity. It is probably of greater importance to give them a purpose for being together forever.

As much as we love our spouses and our children and never want to be apart, we need more. We need a work and something in which to glory. The Lord said, "For behold, this is my work and my glory—to bring to pass the immortality and eternal life of man." (Moses 1:39.)

After a couple are declared husband and wife for eternity, they are immediately blessed with a purpose for being together. If there is greater joy ahead, I cannot comprehend it. And yet, I feel that my grandfather's tears are still not completely understood. I am still, at this writing, not a grandfather.

Some readers may be the only members of the Church in their family. Their parents and grandparents may never have heard about the gospel, let alone accepted it. The temple will provide these individuals with the opportunity for reunions irrespective of which side of the veil their family members are on.

Each of us is commanded to research our family history and personally do the work for our relatives. We are promised feelings of satisfaction, joy, and closeness to the other side as we do so. On occasions where families are sealed together in the holy temple, the veil is very thin and sometimes we are even blessed to have it parted.

Some young people may be the first in their family to join the Church and have the opportunity to lovingly and gently introduce the gospel to other members of the family. Perhaps, however, the greatest opportunity of all will be for them to raise their own children in such a way that someday they can show their grandchildren a picture of their parents, uncles, and aunts in front of a beautiful temple and say, "That was the happiest day of our lives."

Sealing family units for time and all eternity is one of the main functions of our temples. Doing the endowment work for those who left this mortal existence without having experienced these blessings on earth is another. Returning to the temple often on behalf of the dead also allows us to increase our commitment to our own endowment and the covenants we have made.

May I conclude by discussing an element of the endowment that relates to our spiritual progression while on this earth. We often think of the temple ordinance as sealing families together and doing work for the dead. Sometimes we neglect to speak about the spiritual perfecting and sanctifying power that goes on after we receive the endowment.

In the dedicatory prayer for the Kirtland Temple, we

read the following: "And now, Holy Father, we ask . . . that all people who shall enter upon the threshold of the Lord's house may feel thy power. . . . And we ask thee, Holy Father, that thy servants may go forth from this house armed with thy power." (D&C 109:10, 13, 22.)

As part of the endowment, we receive a spiritual power not previously available to us. Elder John A. Widtsoe wrote:

> Modern revelation sets forth the high destiny of those who are sealed for everlasting companionship. They will be given opportunity for a greater use of their powers. That means progress. They will attain more readily to their place in the presence of the Lord; they will increase more rapidly in every divine power; they will approach more nearly to the likeness of God; they will more completely realize their divine destiny. And this progress is not delayed until life after death. It begins here, today, for those who yield obedience to the law. Life is tasteless without progress. Eternal marriage, with all that it means, provides for unending advancement. "Eternal increase" is the gift to all who enter into the eternal marriage covenant, as made in the temples of the Lord. . . .
>
> The men and women who have come with this power out of the Lord's holy house will be hedged about by divine protection and walk more safely among the perplexities of earth. They will be indeed the ultimate conquerors of earth, for they come with the infinite power of God to solve the problems of earth. Spiritual power accompanies all who marry in the temple, if they thenceforth keep their sacred covenants. (*Evidences and Reconciliations* [Salt Lake City: Bookcraft, 1987], pp. 300–301.)

We have been commanded to become perfect even as

our Father in heaven is perfect. Each of us must go through a mighty change. We must be sanctified and purified. As we learn from the people at the time of King Benjamin, this comes about through the Spirit of the Lord Omnipotent. (See Mosiah 5:2.)

We receive the gift of the Holy Ghost after we are baptized and become members of the Church. As we remain true to the covenant, we have access to the promptings of the Holy Ghost, which help us know right from wrong, guide us to eternal truths, and give us direction as we make important decisions in our lives. When we go to the temple, we receive the endowment and more power through the Holy Ghost is given to us, if we remain true to these covenants, that we "may grow up in [God], and receive a fulness of the Holy Ghost, . . . and be prepared to obtain every needful thing." (D&C 109:15.)

Members who go to the temple have access to a fullness of the Holy Ghost that is not available to those who have only received the gift of the Holy Ghost. This is a very real blessing. For example, those who have received their endowments can reflect on the beautiful blessings given at the time they were washed and anointed in the initiatory work. In effect, their body, mind, and soul were dedicated to righteous purposes. I would counsel all to listen carefully to those blessings the next time they perform initiatory work. Great power is given in that part of the endowment.

In King Benjamin's time, the people said: "We have no more disposition to do evil, but to do good continually." (Mosiah 5:2.) Is there a greater power that we can receive in the temple than to conquer our own flesh to the point that our very desires or dispositions are to do only good? It is part of receiving a fullness of the Holy Ghost. As we remain true to our covenants, the sanctification, the purification, and the refining are taking place day in and day out, during temple sessions and between temple visits. That process is an endowment of righteous power, a power to purge ourselves of even the desire to do evil. Once we gain control of our own dispositions, we can become a greater power in the lives of others in assisting the Lord in his mission "to bring to pass the immortality and eternal life of man." (Moses 1:39.)

May we make the endowment active in our lives and allow the sanctifying power of the Holy Ghost to bring about a metamorphosis of our spirits. We need to receive a disposition to do good continually. We need to become celestialized. We need the spiritual revival that can come from participating in temple ordinances and making covenants and then being true and faithful to them.

9

Trials and Tribulations

The greatest protection against the perils of the last days is obedience. However, in spite of our obedience, trials and tribulations will come our way. These are not always for the punishment of the wicked, but often for the sanctification of the righteous.

President Marion G. Romney said, "Latter-day Saints know that much of pain and suffering would be avoided if the people would accept and follow the Savior. Our mission, as a church, is to bring people to a knowledge of Christ and thus avoid all unnecessary suffering. We are aware, however, that should all men accept and live his teachings, adversity and affliction would still abound because, in the words of the Prophet Joseph Smith, 'Men have to suffer that they may come upon Mount Zion and be exalted above the heavens.' (*History of the Church* 5:556.) This does not mean that we crave suffering. We avoid all we can. However, we now know, and we all knew when we elected to come into mortality . . . just as Jesus had to endure affliction to prove himself, so must all men endure affliction to prove themselves." (Conference Report, October 1969, pp. 57–58.)

Into the life of each of us come what I call golden moments of adversity. This may seem like a contradiction of terms. I don't like adversity, tribulations, or pain. I never look for them. In fact, I try very hard to avoid them. However, somewhere, someplace, when I least expect it, there they are, these painful friends that break my heart, drive me to my knees, and make me realize I am nothing without my Lord and Savior. They lead me to petition my Father in prayer all the night long, and into the next day and sometimes for weeks and months. But ultimately, just as surely as the day follows the night, these strange friends lead me straight into the outstretched arms of the Savior.

President Spencer W. Kimball said: "Being human, we would expel from our lives physical pain and mental anguish and assure ourselves of continual ease and comfort, but if we were to close the doors upon sorrow and distress, we might be excluding our greatest friends and benefactors. Suffering can make saints of people as they learn patience, long-suffering, and self-mastery. The sufferings of our Savior were part of his education." (*Faith Precedes the Miracle* [Salt Lake City: Deseret Book, 1974], p. 98.)

At this very moment you, my reader, may be entertaining my friends and could even be in some deep despair. Don't curse them. Don't flee from them by running into forbidden paths and into the outstretched arms of Lucifer. Adversity can be a friend. He gives way to joy when we treat him as a friend and allow him to point us in the right direction.

"Some of the lowliest walks in life, the paths which lead into the deepest valleys of sorrow and up the most rugged steeps of adversity, are the ones which, if a man travel in, will best accomplish the object of his existence in this world," Elder B. H. Roberts wrote. "The conditions which place men where they may always walk on the unbroken plain of prosperity and seek for nothing but their own pleasure, are not the best within the gift of God. For in such circumstances men soon drop into a position analogous to the stagnant pool; while those who have to contend with difficulties, brave dangers, endure disappointments, struggle with sorrows, eat the bread of adversity and drink the water of affliction, develop a moral and spiritual strength, together with a purity of life and character, unknown to the heirs of ease, and wealth, and pleasure. With the English bard, therefore, I believe: Sweet are the uses of adversity!" (*The Gospel: An Exposition of Its Principles* [Salt Lake City: George Q. Cannon and Sons, 1893], pp. 346–47.)

Two comments from President Ezra Taft Benson are pertinent: "While I do not believe in stepping out of the path of duty to pick up a cross I do not need, a man is a coward who refuses to pick up a cross that clearly lies within his path" (Conference Report, April 1967, p. 61), and "It is not on the pinnacle of success and ease where men and women grow most. It is often down in the valley of heartache and disappointment and reverses where men and women grow into strong characters" (Report of the Stockholm Sweden Area Conference, 1974, p. 70).

I like the way Elder Angel Abrea placed afflictions into proper perspective: "Tribulation, afflictions, and trials will constantly be with us in our sojourn here in this segment of eternity. . . . Therefore, the great challenge in this earthly life is not to determine how to escape the afflictions and problems, but rather to carefully prepare ourselves to meet them." (*Ensign,* May 1992, p. 25.)

Elder John B. Dickson recently shared with the priesthood of the Church his feelings about meeting adversity: "I want you to know that having one arm for nearly thirty years has been one of the greatest blessings of my life. It hasn't been my greatest challenge, but it has been a great teacher to me, teaching me to be more patient and tolerant with others as I have had to learn to be more patient with myself. It has helped me to understand the necessity of our having challenges in life to help develop our character and stamina, helping us to become what the Lord ultimately wants us to become.

"Our challenges may be physical, spiritual, economic, or emotional, but if we will treat them as opportunities and stepping-stones in our progress, rather than barriers and stumbling blocks, our lives and growth will be wonderful. I have learned that between challenges it is very restful but that any real growth that I have ever enjoyed has always come with a challenge." (*Ensign,* November 1992, p. 45.)

When we repeat the story of Joseph Smith's First Vision, we often have a tendency to pass over the despair, anxiety, and heartache the Prophet experienced prior to receiving the heavenly visitation. We tell the account something like this: "Joseph Smith was confused about which church to join. One night he was reading the Bible and came upon James 1:5, which tells us if we have a question, we should pray about it. So Joseph went into a grove of trees near his home and he prayed. As he prayed, two messengers appeared before him." Then we go into detail of that beautiful vision.

May I quote the account of what Joseph said happened prior to that vision. I have added italics to some portions to emphasize how he agonized over this experience.

"In the midst of this war of words and tumult of opinions, I often said to myself: *What is to be done?* Who of all these parties are right; or, are they all wrong together? If any one of them be right, which is it, and *how shall I know it?*

"*While I was laboring under the extreme difficulties* caused by the contests of these parties of religionists, I was one day reading the Epistle of James, first chapter and fifth verse. . . .

"*Never* did any passage of scripture come with *more power* to the heart of man than this did at this time to mine. It seemed to enter with *great force* into *every feeling* of my heart. *I reflected on it again and again, knowing that if any person needed wisdom from God, I did; for how to act I did not know, and unless I could get more wisdom than I then had, I would never know;* for the teachers of religion of the different sects understood the same passages of scripture so differently as to destroy all confidence in settling the question by an appeal to the Bible.

"*At length* I came to the conclusion that *I must either remain in darkness and confusion,* or else I must do as James directs, that is, ask of God. I *at length* came to the determination to 'ask of God,' concluding that if he gave wisdom to them that lacked wisdom, and would give liberally, and not upbraid, I might venture.

"So, in accordance with this, my determination to ask of God, I retired to the woods to make the attempt. It was on the morning of a beautiful, clear day, early in the spring of eighteen hundred and twenty. *It was the first time in my life that I had made such an attempt, for amidst all my anxieties I had never as yet made the attempt to pray vocally."*

The hope generated by this breath of fresh air led Joseph to have faith to try something he had never done before. The initial result of this attempt would have been enough for most of us to back off. His reward for this leap of faith was not immediate. In fact, he must have wondered if he was on the wrong path. He continued:

"After I had retired to the place where I had previously designed to go, having looked around me, and finding myself alone, I kneeled down and began to offer up the desires of my heart to God. I had scarcely done so, when *immediately I was seized upon by some power which entirely overcame me, and had such an astonishing influence over me as to bind my tongue so that I could not speak. Thick darkness gathered around me, and it seemed to me for a time as if I were doomed to sudden destruction.*

"But, exerting all my powers to call upon God to deliver me out of the *power of this enemy* which had seized upon me, and *at the very moment when I was ready to sink into despair and abandon myself to destruction — not to an imaginary ruin, but to the power of some actual being from the unseen world, who had such marvelous power as I had never before felt in any being — just at this moment of great alarm,* I saw a pillar of light exactly over my head, above the brightness of the sun, which descended gradually until it fell upon me." (Joseph Smith–History 1:10–16; italics added.)

The answer came when Joseph had exerted all the energy he had. Sometimes we give up at the first sign of trouble or when we don't receive an immediate, clear answer to a sincere prayer.

Later in his life, in 1842, Joseph reflected on many subsequent tribulations: "As for the perils which I am called to pass through, they seem but a small thing to me, as the envy and wrath of man have been my common lot all the days of my life; and for what cause it seems mysterious, unless I was ordained from before the foundation of the world for some good end, or bad, as you may choose to call it. Judge ye for yourselves. God knoweth all these things, whether it be good or bad. But nevertheless, deep water is what I am wont to swim in. It all has become a second nature to me; and I feel, like Paul, to glory in tribulation; for to this day has the God of my fathers delivered me out of them all, and will deliver me from henceforth; for behold, and lo, I shall triumph over all my enemies, for the Lord God hath spoken it." (D&C 127:2.)

Joseph gloried in tribulation, not because he was a masochist but because he knew what was on the horizon or at the end of a storm. He had experienced enough tribulation to know about the rainbows of life. To the Twelve he said: "You will have all kinds of trials to pass through. And it is quite as necessary for you to be tried as it was for Abraham and other men of God, and . . . God will feel after you, and He will take hold of you and wrench your very heart strings, and if you cannot stand it you will not be fit for an inheritance in the Celestial Kingdom of God." (Quoted by John Taylor, *Journal of Discourses* 24:197.)

Brigham Young recognized the good coming from trials. He certainly had his share and learned from them, which led him to say: "Well, do you think that persecution has done us good? Yes. I sit and laugh, and rejoice exceedingly when I see persecution. I care no more about it than I do about the whistling of the north wind, the croaking of the crane that flies over my head, or the crackling of the thorns under the pot. The Lord has all things in his hand; therefore let it come, for it will give me experience." (*Discourses of Brigham Young* [Salt Lake City: Deseret Book, 1954], p. 351.)

John Taylor was also no stranger to adversity. He said, "I rejoice in afflictions, for they are necessary to humble and prove us, that we may comprehend ourselves, become acquainted with our weakness and infirmities; and I rejoice when I triumph over them, because God answers my prayers, therefore I feel to rejoice all the day long." (*Journal of Discourses* 1:17.)

On the subject of Joseph's suffering, Elder Neal A. Maxwell commented:

> Yes, Joseph received remarkable manifestations, along with constant vexations. True, for instance, there were periodic arrivals of heavenly messengers, but these were punctuated by the periodic arrivals of earthly mobs.
>
> While Joseph was befriended by heavenly notables, he was also betrayed by some of his earthly friends. Receiving keys and gifts was real, but so was the painful loss of six of the eleven children born to him and Emma. Granted, Joseph had revealed to him glimpses of far horizons—the first and third estates. But these periodic glories occurred amid Joseph's arduous, daily life in the second estate. . . .
>
> Concerning his personal suffering, Joseph was promised, "Thy heart shall be enlarged." An enlarged Joseph wrote from Liberty Jail, "It seems to me that my heart will always be more tender after this than ever it was before. . . . I think I never could have felt as I now do if I had not suffered." (*The Personal Writings of Joseph*

Smith, ed. Dean C. Jessee [Salt Lake City: Deseret Book, 1984], p. 387.) Was Joseph not told, "All these things shall give thee experience, and shall be for thy good"? (D&C 122:7.) (*Ensign,* May 1992, pp. 38–39.)

The scriptures are full of examples in which the greatest spiritual moments were preceded by the darkest hours. Enos expressed despair and hungered for the love of the Lord prior to knowing his sins had been forgiven: "I will tell you of the wrestle which I had before God, before I received a remission of my sins.

"Behold, I went to hunt beasts in the forests; and the words which I had often heard my father speak concerning eternal life, and the joy of the saints, sunk deep into my heart. And my soul hungered; and I kneeled down before my Maker, and I cried unto him in mighty prayer and supplication for mine own soul; and all the day long did I cry unto him; yea, and when the night came I did still raise my voice high that it reached the heavens. And there came a voice unto me, saying: Enos, thy sins are forgiven thee, and thou shalt be blessed. And I, Enos, knew that God could not lie; wherefore, my guilt was swept away." (Enos 1:2–6.)

The sons of Mosiah, we are told, suffered before they were comforted: "Now these are the circumstances which attended them in their journeyings, for they had many afflictions; they did suffer much, both in body and in mind, such as hunger, thirst and fatigue, and also much labor in the spirit. . . . And it came to pass that the Lord did visit them with his Spirit, and said unto them: Be comforted. And they were comforted." (Alma 17:5, 10.)

Nephi, the son of Helaman, received his beautiful promise and comfort at the hour of his deepest despair:

"It came to pass that there arose a division among the people, insomuch that they divided hither and thither and went their ways, leaving Nephi alone, as he was standing in the midst of them.

"And it came to pass that Nephi went his way towards his own house, pondering upon the things which the Lord had shown unto him. And it came to pass as he was thus pondering—being much cast down because of the wickedness of the people of the Nephites, their secret works of darkness, and their murderings, and their plunderings, and all manner of iniquities—and it came to pass as he was thus pondering in his heart, behold, a voice came unto him saying: Blessed art thou, Nephi, for those things which thou hast done." (Helaman 10:1–4.)

Alma was at rock bottom when the same angel who had called him to repentance earlier in his life returned to give him comfort:

"Now when the people had said this, and withstood all his words, and reviled him, and spit upon him, and caused that he should be cast out of their city, he departed thence and took his journey towards the city which was called Aaron.

"And it came to pass that while he was journeying thither, being weighed down with sorrow, wading through much tribulation and anguish of soul, because of the wickedness of the people who were in the city of Ammonihah, it came to pass while Alma was thus weighed down with sorrow, behold an angel of the Lord appeared unto him, saying: Blessed art thou, Alma; therefore, lift up thy head and rejoice, for thou hast great cause to rejoice; for thou hast been faithful in keeping the commandments of God from the time which thou receivedst thy first mes-

sage from him. Behold, I am he that delivered it unto you."
(Alma 8:13–15.)

It seems to be the rule rather than the exception that
the storm precedes the calm, beautiful day. An interesting
example of this phenomenon occurred when eight of the
first twelve apostles of this dispensation were included in
Zion's Camp, an experience that was full of tribulation.
Without subsequent insight, those participating might
even have felt it was a failure.

From this perspective, we can see why the Saints will
not escape all trials and tribulations even if they are obedient. At times it may seem that we receive more trials
than those who are living in and of the world.

Elder Bruce R. McConkie said: "Sometimes the tests
and trials of those who have received the gospel far exceed
any imposed upon worldly people. Abraham was called
upon to sacrifice his only son. Lehi and his family left their
lands and wealth to live in a wilderness. Saints in all ages
have been commanded to lay all that they have upon the
altar, sometimes even their very lives. As to the individual
trials [or] problems that befall any of us, all we need say
is that in the wisdom of Him who knows all things, and
who does all the things well, all of us are given the particular and specific tests that we need in our personal situations." (Conference Report, October 1976, p. 158.)

It is interesting to note that with the increased ills of
a wicked society have come society's ways of dealing with
the adversity that accompanies them. We live in a society
where pain of any kind is unacceptable; therefore, when
we begin to feel a symptom, we immediately turn to the
painkiller. We sometimes turn away from the very battle
that could strengthen and sanctify us. We give lip service

to the scripture, "For it must needs be, that there is an opposition in all things" (2 Nephi 2:11), but our hearts are not in it and we would much rather eliminate adversity than meet it and conquer it. We find that what the Church teaches and what has become the norm in society are different. Rather than dig down deep within ourselves and find the testimony and the strength to rise above the pointing fingers of a failing society, we have a tendency to join them.

Few of us aren't battling our own goliaths. The battle often takes place so deeply within us it can only be touched by the Spirit. Rather than cursing the situation in which we find ourselves and asking, "What did I ever do to deserve this," perhaps we should consider the possibility that the adversity we face is for our eternal growth. Perhaps a particular goliath has come along because of the many things we have done right.

With hindsight, we look back at the early Saints' experiences in Zion's Camp, the Missouri and Nauvoo expulsions, and the trek west as just what was needed to raise up the people to be prepared to build Zion. Future generations may look upon our particular period in time and say that the challenges we faced were just what we needed to spiritually prepare us to take the kingdom to its next plateau to survive the trials ahead.

The recurring theme of the Book of Mormon is that as long as the people were faithful, they were prosperous. However, when they became prosperous and comfortable, there was a tendency to let down and become disobedient. Therefore, the Lord sent them adversity as a wake-up call. "And thus we see that except the Lord doth chasten his people with many afflictions, yea, except he doth visit them with death and with terror, and with famine and with all manner of pestilence, they will not remember him." (Helaman 12:3.)

Nephi, who understood this principle, actually prayed for a famine. He felt that a famine was better than having the Spirit of the Lord withdraw because of wickedness. He knew the people could not be upheld in battle without being righteous, and so he prayed, "O Lord, do not suffer that this people shall be destroyed by the sword; but O Lord, rather let there be a famine in the land, to stir them up in remembrance of the Lord their God, and perhaps they will repent and turn unto thee." (Helaman 11:4.)

In our dispensation the Lord has revealed a similar principle: "My people must needs be chastened until they learn obedience, if it must needs be, by the things which they suffer." (D&C 105:6.)

Disasters of the last days were put into the proper perspective by President Joseph F. Smith: "We believe that these severe, natural calamities are visited upon men by the Lord for the good of his children, to quicken their devotion to others, and to bring out their better natures, that they may love and serve him. We believe, further, that they are the heralds and tokens of his final judgment, and the schoolmasters to teach the people to prepare themselves by righteous living for the coming of the Savior to reign upon the earth, when every knee shall bow and every tongue confess that Jesus is the Christ." (*Gospel Doctrine*, p. 55.)

Sometimes it is enough to make one want to be less spiritual and more comfortable. Often it appears the nonbelievers are having all the fun. However, despite trials and tribulations, our highs are higher and our joys are

greater than are those of individuals who escape the re-
finer's fire. Don't mistake telestial happiness for celestial
joy. We don't have to die in order to receive this joy beyond
description.

Alma provides this contrast on pain and joy: "And it
came to pass that as I was thus racked with torment, while
I was harrowed up by the memory of my many sins, behold, I remembered also to have heard my father prophesy
unto the people concerning the coming of one Jesus Christ,
a Son of God, to atone for the sins of the world.

"Now, as my mind caught hold upon this thought, I
cried within my heart: O Jesus, thou Son of God, have
mercy on me, who am in the gall of bitterness, and am
encircled about by the everlasting chains of death.

"And now, behold, when I thought this, I could remember my pains no more; yea, I was harrowed up by
the memory of my sins no more.

"And oh, what joy, and what marvelous light I did
behold; yea, my soul was filled with joy as exceeding as
was my pain! Yea, . . . there could be nothing so exquisite
and so bitter as were my pains. . . . [and] on the other
hand, there can be nothing so exquisite and sweet as was
my joy." (Alma 36:17–21.)

I have tried to understand why we must experience
tribulation before we can experience the ultimate communication. President Kimball said, "When man begins to
hunger, when arms begin to reach, when knees begin to
bend and voices begin to articulate, then, and not until
then, does the Lord make himself known. He pushes back
the horizons, he breaks the curtain above us, and he makes
it possible for us to come out of dim, uncertain stumbling

into the sureness of the eternal light." (*Teachings of Spencer W. Kimball* [Salt Lake City: Bookcraft, 1982], pp. 453–54.)

On the same subject, Elder Maxwell said: "Only greater consecration will cure ambivalence and casualness in any of us! . . . The tutoring challenges arising from increased consecration may be severe but reflect the divine mercy necessary to induce further consecration. (See Hel. 12:3.) If we have grown soft, hard times may be necessary. Deprivation may prepare us for further consecration, though we shudder at the thought. If we are too easily contented, God may administer a dose of divine discontent." (*Ensign*, November 1992, p. 66.)

We are living in the last days now. There is no time to wait for things to get worse before we get on the train. Each member of the Church has a role to play in the rolling forth of the kingdom. This book is a plea for help in that regard. A spiritual revival is needed in order that our trials in these latter days may be met and overcome. Each victory will make us stronger for future trials as well as make us more effective in helping the Lord roll out his kingdom in this most exciting but challenging time.

Each of us has had our share of adversity. I myself am no stranger to it. If we will turn upward in our hours of need, the Lord will comfort us. Of this I bear witness. The storm will subside for a season. None of us will be tested beyond our endurance. Each triumph takes our spirituality to a higher plateau. When valleys get lower, our peaks get higher. We can continue until we obtain that ultimate victory of returning home to that Father who gave us life and to that Brother who offers us the hope of eternal life with them both. May we be blessed in our journey.

10

Commitment and Sacrifice

In building the kingdom and for our individual spirituality, sacrifice is a must. We usually think of sacrifice as being associated with obedience. When we are committed, we are willing and anxious to sacrifice, and sacrifice brings forth the blessings of heaven.

In the train analogy on page 2, I talked about three types of people: those who get on and off the train as they please, those who run alongside the train but refuse to get on, and those who think they are wise enough to run ahead of the train. All three types of people lack full commitment, and if each type would increase his or her commitment, everyone would stay on the train.

In the same general conference where I gave my "Spiritual Revival" talk, Elder Neal A. Maxwell gave a talk in which he referred to "casual discipleship." The following excerpts not only help support my train analogy but also do so through the eloquence of Elder Maxwell:

147

Eighteen years ago from this same pulpit, I pled with those who stood indecisively on the "porch" of the Church to come fully inside. (See *Ensign,* Nov. 1974, pp. 12–13.) Today, my plea is to those members already inside but whose discipleship is casual, individuals whom we love, whose gifts and talents are much needed in building the kingdom!

Any call for greater consecration is, of course, really a call to all of us. But these remarks are not primarily for those who are steadily striving and who genuinely seek to keep God's commandments and yet sometimes fall short. (D&C 46:9.) Nor is this primarily for those few in deliberate noncompliance, including some who cast off on intellectual and behavioral bungee cords in search of new sensations, only to be jerked about by the old heresies and the old sins.

Instead, these comments are for the essentially "honorable" members who are skimming over the surface instead of deepening their discipleship and who are casually engaged rather than "anxiously engaged." (D&C 76:75; 58:27.) Though nominal in their participation, their reservations and hesitations inevitably show through. They may even pass through our holy temples but, alas, they do not let the holy temples pass through them. . . .

Some of these otherwise honorable members mistakenly regard the Church as an institution, but not as a kingdom. They know the doctrines of the kingdom, but more as a matter of recitation than of real comprehension. . . . Each of us is an innkeeper who decides if there is room for Jesus! (*Ensign,* November 1992, pp. 65–66.)

The same point is made in Revelation 3:15–20:

"I know thy works, that thou art neither cold nor hot: I would thou wert cold or hot. So then because thou art lukewarm, and neither cold nor hot, I will spue thee out of my mouth.

"Because thou sayest, I am rich, and increased with goods, and have need of nothing; and knowest not that thou art wretched, and miserable, and poor, and blind, and naked: I counsel thee to buy of me gold tried in the fire, that thou mayest be rich; and white raiment, that thou mayest be clothed, and that the shame of thy nakedness do not appear; and anoint thine eyes with eyesalve, that thou mayest see.

"As many as I love, I rebuke and chasten: be zealous therefore, and repent. Behold, I stand at the door, and knock: if any man hear my voice, and open the door, I will come in to him, and will sup with him, and he with me."

Without unwavering commitment, it is impossible to receive unwavering faith. When we know we are falling short, we are incapable of asking things of the Lord with confidence. Without sacrifice, our asking is also somewhat hollow. Receiving additional spiritual knowledge as individuals depends on our commitment and sacrifice. This condition is disclosed in the Doctrine and Covenants, where the Lord commends Parley P. Pratt for his efforts in the Church's school in Missouri:

"I will bless him [Elder Pratt] with a multiplicity of blessings, in expounding all scriptures and mysteries to the edification of the school, and of the church in Zion. . . . Verily I say unto you, all . . . who know their hearts are honest, and are broken, and their spirits contrite, and are willing to observe their covenants by sacrifice—yea, every sacrifice which I, the Lord, shall command—they are accepted of me. For I, the Lord, will cause them to bring forth as a very fruitful tree which is planted in a goodly land, by a pure stream, that yieldeth much precious fruit." (D&C 97:5, 8–9.)

In "Lectures on Faith," a series of discussions prepared by the Prophet Joseph Smith for delivery to the School of the Prophets in Kirtland, Ohio, we learn of a relationship between faith, testimony, commitment, sacrifice, and the reception of blessings:

> [Lecture 1, no. 55] Let us here observe, that after any portion of the human family are made acquainted with the important fact that there is a God, who has created and does uphold all things, the extent of their knowledge respecting his character and glory will depend upon their diligence [or commitment] and faithfulness in seeking after him, until, like Enoch, the brother of Jared, and Moses, they shall obtain faith in God, and power with him to behold him face to face.

When we have received a testimony that there is a God, we move forward with faith to learn more. We do so with diligence, or commitment, until all things can be made known.

> [Lecture 1, no. 56] We have now clearly set forth how it is, and how it was, that God became an object of faith for rational beings; and also, upon what foundation the testimony was based which excited the inquiry and diligent [committed] search of the ancient saints to seek after and obtain a knowledge of the glory of God; and we have seen that it was human testimony, and human testimony only, that excited this inquiry, in the first instance, in their minds. It was the credence they gave to the testimony of their fathers, this testimony having aroused their minds to inquire after the knowledge of God; the inquiry frequently terminated, indeed

always terminated when rightly pursued, in the most glorious discoveries and eternal certainty.

[Lecture 6, no. 7] Let us here observe, that a religion that does not require the sacrifice of all things never has power sufficient to produce the faith necessary unto life and salvation; for, from the first existence of man, the faith necessary unto the enjoyment of life and salvation never could be obtained without the sacrifice of all earthly things. It was through this sacrifice, and this only, that God has ordained that men should enjoy eternal life; and it is through the medium of the sacrifice of all earthly things that men do actually know that they are doing the things that are well pleasing in the sight of God. When a man has offered in sacrifice all that he has for the truth's sake, not even withholding his life, and believing before God that he has been called to make this sacrifice because he seeks to do his will, he does know, most assuredly, that God does and will accept his sacrifice and offering, and that he has not, nor will not seek his face in vain. Under these circumstances, then, he can obtain the faith necessary for him to lay hold on eternal life.

[Lecture 6, no. 10] Those, then, who make the sacrifice, will have the testimony that their course is pleasing in the sight of God; and those who have this testimony will have faith to lay hold on eternal life, and will be enabled, through faith, to endure unto the end, and receive the crown that is laid up for them that love the appearing of our Lord Jesus Christ. But those who do not make the sacrifice cannot enjoy this faith, because men are dependent upon this sacrifice in order to obtain this faith: therefore, they cannot lay hold upon eternal life, because the revelations of God do not guarantee unto them the authority so to do, and without this guarantee faith could not exist. (*Lectures on Faith* [Salt Lake City: Deseret Book, 1985], pp. 24, 69, 70.)

These quotations may seem rather heavy, but the message is relatively simple as an explanation of how faith, testimony, commitment, sacrifice, and receipt of blessing fit together. We receive a testimony of the reality of the existence of God the Father and his Son, Jesus Christ. This gives us the faith to communicate with the Father through the Son in prayer, and should also motivate us to be committed and willing to sacrifice our worldly possessions and desires as he asks us. The knowledge that we are willing to sacrifice all gives us a power and confidence called faith. And when we use the power of faith, we can obtain hidden treasures of higher knowledge and eternal life itself.

Two quotations from President George Q. Cannon explain quite clearly the blessings that come from sacrifice:

"In the revelations of the Lord given to the Church in our day are many commandments which the Saints are required to observe, and accompanying these commandments are most glorious promises to all who will obey; and if it requires any sacrifice on our part to observe these laws, the reward that follows is a hundred-fold recompense for such sacrifice." (*Gospel Truth*, p. 124.)

"I say to you this day, in the presence of God and the holy angels and of this assembly, if we expect to attain the fulfillment of the promises God has made to us, we must be self-sacrificing. There is no sacrifice that God can ask of us or His servants whom He has chosen to lead us that we should hesitate about making. In one sense of the word it is no sacrifice. We may call it so because it comes in contact with our selfishness and our unbelief; but it ought not to come in contact with our faith." (*Gospel Truth*, p. 89.)

The necessity and rewards of commitment and sacrifice

are illustrated in a personal experience I had in Aba, Nigeria. Shortly after my call to the Presiding Bishopric, I visited Nigeria and Ghana on a welfare assignment. There I traveled with the mission president, who was kind enough to orient me and teach me. Everything went smoothly until, on Thursday, he announced he had scheduled a district leadership meeting for Sunday afternoon.

The reason for my anxiety was that the district covered a radius of about fifty miles. That may not seem very far to those living in the United States, but can you imagine what fifty miles means in Nigeria? Some members would have to travel a full day, in 90 degree temperature and 90 percent humidity, on crowded buses that stopped every block to let people on, let people off, break down—or all of the above. Their bus travel would also be at the expense of food money. Those who lived closer and were blessed to own bicycles might pedal for several hours. Some people would have to walk.

Knowing of these sacrifices, I was a little upset with the mission president and suggested that he cancel the meeting. He gave me a frustrated look and asked, "How would you suggest we contact them, drums? Today's Thursday and there's no way we can reach the members and call off this meeting by Sunday. And besides that, let me tell you something. They are not coming to see you—they are coming to see a General Authority."

This was a good lesson to me. I had been a General Authority for only a few months and hadn't quite got used to the fact that I was more than just Glenn now. Of course, I realized the meeting would have to be held. However, that didn't allay my anxiety about it. Put yourself in my place: People are coming long distances and at great inconvenience, both financially and physically, to see you. What are you going to tell them that would be worth their sacrifice? I have never worried more about what I would present than I did about that meeting. Speaking in general conference brought me less anxiety. I fretted and stewed. I fasted and prayed. I didn't know their culture. I didn't know the depth of their gospel knowledge or their spirituality. All I knew was that they were coming with excitement and great anticipation to see and listen to a General Authority, and I was he.

Sunday arrived. I had decided to talk about some lesser known experiences of Joseph Smith, as an approach to bear witness of his role in the Restoration. The people were attentive and polite, but I didn't feel I was rewarding them for their sacrifice. Suddenly, as I was bearing my testimony, in mid-sentence I had an impression that came in the form of a memory. I paused for a moment, and then asked, "Who is the President of the Church today?"

I fully expected them to answer "Spencer W. Kimball," since Ezra Taft Benson had been the prophet for only three months, and some of these members lived in very isolated settings. However, a man on the front row stood tall and erect and replied, "Ezra Taft Benson."

I told them that I doubted President Benson would ever be able to come to Aba, Nigeria. "He is nearing ninety years of age," I explained. "I am only forty-five and this trip has just about done me in." They chuckled at that, but then they got very sad to think they might never see the prophet.

I continued (and this was the memory in the impression), "However, do you know that just ten days ago I was in the same room with him and was as close to him as I am to your district president? I told him I was coming to Nigeria and Ghana and he said, 'Can I come?' I looked at Presidents Hinckley and Monson and they were shaking their heads. He looked at them, smiled, and said, 'I guess not. But Bishop, will you tell them hello for me and that I love them?' "

The members' eyes got as big as saucers, and big smiles came to their faces. Some had tears streaming down their cheeks, just to know they were looking at a person who had been with the prophet. Furthermore, the prophet had sent them a greeting. I was totally unprepared for their reaction.

After regaining my composure, I continued. "As a matter of fact, next Friday I will be with him again. If any of you would like to shake my hand, I will stand at the back door after this meeting, and when I get home I will pass along your handshake to the prophet."

I might as well have stopped talking, and soon did, because they were looking back at the door, shuffling their feet, and some even started to line up. After the meeting, I stood for an hour because not one of the approximately fifty people in attendance left without coming to shake my hand. They not only shook my hand, but each one had a message:

"Tell the prophet we love him."

"Tell the prophet I've read the Book of Mormon."

"Tell the prophet I don't smoke anymore."

One person said, "Tell the prophet I don't hit my wife anymore" and I replied, "He'll be most happy to hear that."

As I have returned to that district (which is now two stakes) each year since that time, many members will come to me and say, "I was at the meeting." "The meeting," I have since learned, was where, through the Spirit, they were given a brief visit with the prophet.

A year later, I went to Ghana and was asked to speak in a branch sacrament meeting where about 150 people were in attendance. Remembering my experience in Nigeria, I felt no anxiety and made no special preparation for this meeting. I knew what worked and gave the same message. The response? Nothing. Flat. Blank stares.

Afterwards the mission president drove me back to his home, and I went into my room to lick my wounds. I felt awful. I felt as if I had let these Saints down. I didn't feel the mantle and, consequently, I didn't think I had been able to convey it to them. I lay on my back, watching the lizards run across the walls, and wondered why I had failed. Why had there been such an outpouring of the Spirit in Nigeria and not in Ghana? After much anguish and prayer, I learned the reason. Into my mind came a gentle but powerful truth: "The difference was sacrifice: yours and theirs." I knew that was true.

None of the elements I've discussed earlier in this chapter were present, at least to me. There was no deep commitment, no sacrifice; and because of that lack of preparation, the prayer I had offered prior to speaking lacked the faith necessary to call down the powers of heaven.

A moving sermon on this subject was delivered by President Gordon B. Hinckley on Sunday, October 6, 1991. He described the hardships suffered by some of the handcart companies, recounted how many died of exposure, and told the story of two girls who lost their parents on the trail. I pick up his account with the last part of their story, as President Hinckley told it:

The two orphan girls, Maggie and Ellen, were among those with frozen limbs. Ellen's were the most serious. The doctor in the valley, doing the best he could, amputated her legs just below the knees. The surgical tools were crude. There was no anesthesia. The stumps never healed. She grew to womanhood, married William Unthank, and bore and reared an honorable family of six children. Moving about on those stumps, she served her family, her neighbors, and the Church with faith and good cheer, and without complaint, though she was never without pain. Her posterity are numerous, and among them are educated and capable men and women who love the Lord whom she loved and who love the cause for which she suffered.

Years later, a group in Cedar City were talking about her and others who were in those ill-fated companies. Members of the group spoke critically of the Church and its leaders because the company of converts had been permitted to start so late in the season. I now quote from a manuscript which I have:

"One old man in the corner sat silent and listened as long as he could stand it. Then he arose and said things that no person who heard will ever forget. His face was white with emotion, yet he spoke calmly, deliberately, but with great earnestness and sincerity.

"He said in substance, 'I ask you to stop this criticism. You are discussing a matter you know nothing about. Cold historic facts mean nothing here for they give no proper interpretation of the questions involved. A mistake to send the handcart company out so late in the season? Yes. But I was in that company and my wife was in it and Sister Nellie Unthank whom you have cited was there too. We suffered beyond anything you can imagine and many died of exposure and starvation, but did you ever hear a survivor of that company utter a word of criticism? Not one of that company ever apostatized or left the church because every one of us came through with the absolute knowledge that God lives for we became acquainted with him in our extremities.' " (*Ensign*, November 1991, p. 54.)

Relative to this account and other similar episodes where the Saints suffered so much, Elder James E. Faust suggested the reason and need for sacrifice:

> I cannot help wondering why these intrepid pioneers had to pay for their faith with such a terrible price in agony and suffering. Why were not the elements tempered to spare them from their profound agony? I believe their lives were consecrated to a higher purpose through their suffering. Their love for the Savior was burned deep in their souls, and into the souls of their children, and their children's children. The motivation for their lives came from a true conversion in the center of their souls. As President Gordon B. Hinckley has said, "When there throbs in the heart of an individual Latter-day Saint a great and vital testimony of the truth of this work, he will be found doing his duty in the Church." (*Ensign*, May 1984, p. 99.)
>
> Above and beyond the epic historical events they participated in, the pioneers found a guide to personal living. They found reality and meaning in their lives. In the difficult days of their journey, the members of the Martin and Willie handcart companies encountered some apostates from the Church who were returning from the West, going back to the East. These apostates tried to persuade some in the companies to turn back. A few did turn back. But the great majority of the pioneers went forward to a heroic achievement in this life, and to eternal life in the life hereafter. (*Ensign*, November 1992, p. 85.)

The ultimate sacrifice brought to pass the ultimate relationship with the Savior. What about us today? What are our avenues of sacrifice? We may never be called upon to die for the kingdom, but each of us must be so committed that we would be willing to do it. Perhaps in the long run, living for the kingdom is more difficult.

President Hinckley gave us all a challenge for today: "If we are to build that Zion of which the prophets have spoken and of which the Lord has given mighty promise, we must set aside our consuming selfishness. We must rise above our love for comfort and ease, and in the very process of effort and struggle, even in our extremity, we shall become better acquainted with our God. Let us never forget that we have a marvelous heritage received from great and courageous people who endured unimaginable suffering and demonstrated unbelievable courage for the cause they loved. You and I know what we should do." (*Ensign,* November 1991, p. 59.)

Elder M. Russell Ballard said, "Our commitment to the kingdom should match that of our faithful ancestors even though our sacrifices are different. They were driven from comfortable homes and compelled to journey one thousand miles by ox-drawn wagon and handcart to reestablish their families, homes, and Church in safety. Our sacrifices may be more subtle but no less demanding. Instead of physical deprivation and hardship, we face the challenge of remaining true and faithful to gospel principles amidst such evil and destructive forces as dishonesty, corruption, drug and alcohol misuse, and disease often caused by sexual promiscuity. Also, we find ourselves in combat daily with immorality in all of its many forms. Pornography and violence, often portrayed in insidious television shows, movies, and videos, are running rampant. Hate and envy, greed and selfishness are all about us, and families are disintegrating at an ever-increasing pace." (*Ensign,* May 1992, p. 75.)

Yes, we need to have a revival in our commitment and to be willing to sacrifice that which is needed for the Lord's sake. As we do so, our testimonies will deepen below the surface and we will gain the confidence and faith to receive the personal revelation and communication we need to make our way through this life to life eternal.

11

Strengthening
Our Testimony

I believe the time has come for all of us to feast on the fruit of our own testimony as opposed to the testimony of another person. The testimony of which I speak is much deeper than knowing the Church is true. We need to progress to the point of knowing we are true to the Church.

A few years ago, my wife and I were standing on land in Nauvoo, Illinois, that was owned by my great-great-grandparents. My great-great-grandfather died at age forty, about the time of Joseph Smith's martyrdom, leaving my great-great-grandmother alone to walk the plains to the Great Salt Lake in 1848. I wondered on that occasion if I had the spirituality to do what she did. Then the question shifted from "Could I have endured what she did?" to "Can I endure what is currently facing me and what lies ahead?" We often wonder if we could have endured the past. It is time to ask ourselves if we are measuring up in our present situations and if we are spiritually prepared for tomorrow.

It is vital that we know that Jesus is the Christ, Joseph Smith is a prophet, the Book of Mormon is the word of God, and Ezra Taft Benson is a prophet. These witnesses are all necessary, important, and beautiful. However, our testimonies must reach a new level. For example, each of us might well ask: Do I have a testimony of my role in building the kingdom? Does God love me? Am I on the right path? Have I been forgiven of my transgressions? Am I receiving personal revelation to guide my own life?

It is one thing to receive a witness that Joseph Smith saw God and Christ. I received that testimony when I was ten years old. It is quite another thing to have spiritual self-confidence in our own ability to receive revelation and act on it when counterfeit voices are all around us.

Sooner or later, and usually both, we are tested. Our confidence in ourselves and in the gospel will be shaken to the core. We must pull out our foundation, if it has been built in the sand of someone else's testimony, and build a new foundation on the rocks of our own testimony and ability to receive revelation. Then, when the storm comes, we can stand no matter who may fall around us.

Many Latter-day Saints are so caught up in projecting what they must prepare for in the future that they fail to realize we are now living in the last days and we are not adequately dealing with today's problems. If we are not coping well with today, how can we expect to be prepared for tomorrow? Over the past few years, we have seen many prophecies come to pass, both glorious and frightening. The growth of the Church has been phenomenal both in numbers of people and in the opening of new countries. On the other hand, the whole world is in commotion with atrocities taking place all around us. Satan is in a rage. But while the world is in commotion, the kingdom is intact.

With all the prophesies we have seen fulfilled in the last few years, what are we waiting for? What great event are we awaiting prior to saying, "Count me in"? What more do we need to see or experience before we get on the train and stay on until we reach our destination of exaltation with our Father in heaven and our Savior, Jesus Christ?

In the book *Life of Heber C. Kimball,* a man named John Nicholson reported that in a speech given in 1867, President Kimball stated that "there were many within hearing who had often wished that they had been associated with the Prophet Joseph. 'You imagine,' said [President Kimball], 'that you would have stood by him when persecution raged and he was assailed by foes within and without. You would have defended him and been true to him in the midst of every trial. You think you would have been delighted to have shown your integrity in the days of mobs and traitors.

" 'Let me say to you, that many of you will see the time when you will have all the trouble, trial and persecution that you can stand, and plenty of opportunities to show that you are true to God and his work. This Church has before it many close places through which it will have to pass before the work of God is crowned with victory. To meet the difficulties that are coming, it will be necessary for you to have a knowledge of the truth of this work for yourselves. The difficulties will be of such a character that the man or woman who does not possess this personal

knowledge or witness will fall. If you have not got the
testimony, live right and call upon the Lord and cease not
till you obtain it. If you do not you will not stand. . . .

" 'The time will come when no man or woman will be
able to endure on borrowed light. Each will have to be
guided by the light within himself. If you do not have it,
how can you stand?' " (Orson F. Whitney, *Life of Heber C.
Kimball,* reprint ed. [Salt Lake City: Bookcraft, 1945], pp.
449–50.)

Reading this was like reading a page out of my own
journal. Many years ago I took the occasion to read the
History of the Church. At the conclusion of the exercise, I
too fantasized about how valiant I would have been had
I lived at the time of Joseph Smith. The Spirit brought me
up short during one of those fantasies. It was made known
to me that if by some miracle I were to be taken back to
live my life at the time of Joseph and Hyrum and all I could
take with me was my current spirituality, I would not have
been successful. This knowledge cut me to the quick. I
would have died for Joseph Smith, but don't ask me to
take any more than two home teaching families. I would
have died for Joseph Smith, but don't ask me to do anything I don't really want to do. I would have died for Joseph
Smith, but what was I doing for Spencer W. Kimball?

Heber C. Kimball explained, "Yes, . . . we think we
are secure here in the chambers of the everlasting hills,
where we can close those few doors of the canyons against
mobs and persecutors, the wicked and the vile, who have
always beset us with violence and robbery, but I want to
say to you, my brethren [and sisters], the time is coming
when we will be mixed up in these now peaceful valleys
to the extent that it will be difficult to tell the face of a

Saint from the face of an enemy to the people of God. Then, brethren [and sisters], look out for the great sieve, for there will be a great sifting time, and many will fall; for I say unto you there is a *test*, a TEST, a TEST coming, and who will be able to stand?" (*Life of Heber C. Kimball*, p. 446.)

It is my testimony that we are well into the beginning of the fulfillment of this prophecy, and yet what we are experiencing is only the beginning of what lies ahead. It is naive to think Lucifer will allow us to live in peace and serenity as we keep an eye on the heavens waiting for the Savior's triumphant return. Prior to that ultimate triumph, we will be tested to the maximum, and perhaps the greatest test will come from within rather than from without the Church. The greatest battle to be fought by us as individuals may be fought as an inner struggle, as opposed to anything that can be inflicted upon us from without.

On this subject President Joseph F. Smith said: "One fault to be avoided by the Saints, young and old, is the tendency to live on borrowed light, with their own hidden under a bushel; to permit the savor of their salt of knowledge to be lost; and the light within them to be reflected, rather than original. . . . Men and women should become settled in the truth, and founded in the knowledge of the gospel, depending upon no person for borrowed or reflected light, but trusting only upon the Holy Spirit, who is ever the same, shining forever and testifying to the individual and the priesthood, who live in harmony with the laws of the gospel, of the glory and the will of the Father. They will then have light everlasting which cannot be obscured." (*Gospel Doctrine*, p. 87.)

Brigham Young, in his usual plainness, said: "Those

men, or those women, who know no more about the power of God, and the influences of the Holy Spirit, than to be led entirely by another person, suspending their own understanding, and pinning their faith upon another's sleeve, will never be capable of entering into the celestial glory, to be crowned as they anticipate; they will never be capable of becoming Gods. They cannot rule themselves, to say nothing of ruling others, but they must be dictated to in every trifle, like a child. . . . They never can hold sceptres of glory, majesty, and power in the celestial kingdom. Who will? Those who are valiant and inspired with the true independence of heaven, who will go forth boldly in the service of their God, leaving others to do as they please, determined to do right, though all mankind besides should take the opposite course." (*Journal of Discourses* 1:312.)

This same truth was taught by President Harold B. Lee: "The time is here when each of you must stand on your own feet. Be converted, because no one can endure on borrowed light. You will have to be guided by the light within yourself. If you do not have it, you will not stand." (*Stand Ye in Holy Places* [Salt Lake City: Deseret Book, 1974], p. 95.)

Perhaps two more quotations will summarize the process of gaining a basic testimony. Elder Bruce R. McConkie wrote:

> Three great truths must be included in every valid testimony: 1. That Jesus Christ is the Son of God and the Savior of the world (D&C 46:13); 2. That Joseph Smith is the Prophet of God through whom the gospel was restored in this dispensation; and 3. That The Church of Jesus Christ of Latter-day Saints is "the only true and living church upon the face of the whole earth." (D&C 1:30.) . . .

Any accountable person can gain a testimony of the gospel by obedience to that law upon which the receipt of such knowledge is predicated. This is the formula: 1. He must *desire* to know the truth of the gospel, of the Book of Mormon, of the Church, or of whatever is involved. 2. He must *study* and learn the basic facts relative to the matter involved. "Search the scriptures." (John 5:39.) "Search these commandments." (D&C 1:37.) 3. He must *practice* the principles and truths learned, conforming his life to them. "My doctrine is not mine, but his that sent me. If any man will do his will, he shall know of the doctrine, whether it be of God, or whether I speak of myself." (John 7:16–17.) 4. He must *pray* to the Father in the name of Christ, *in faith,* and the truth will then be made manifest by revelation "by the power of the Holy Ghost. And by the power of the Holy Ghost ye may know the truth of all things." (Moro. 10:3–5; 1 Cor. 2.) (*Mormon Doctrine* [Salt Lake City: Bookcraft, 1966], pp. 786–87.)

And as expressed by Joseph F. Smith:

When I as a boy first started out in the ministry, I would frequently go out and ask the Lord to show me some marvelous thing, in order that I might receive a testimony. But the Lord withheld marvels from me, and showed me the truth, line upon line, precept upon precept, here a little and there a little, until he made me to know the truth from the crown of my head to the soles of my feet, and until doubt and fear had been absolutely purged from me. He did not have to send an angel from the heavens to do this, nor did he have to speak with the trump of an archangel. By the whisperings of the still small voice of the Spirit of the living God, he gave to me the testimony I possess. And by this principle and power he will give to all the children of men a knowledge of the truth that will stay with them, and it will make them to know the truth, as God knows it, and to do the will of the Father as Christ does it. And no amount of marvelous manifestations will ever accomplish this. It is obedience, humility, and submission to the requirements of heaven and to the order established in the kingdom of God upon the earth, that will establish men in the truth. (*Gospel Doctrine,* p. 7.)

If we don't yet have that basic testimony, when do we begin? It is an understatement to declare that the time of preparation is upon us. The luxury of the "wait and see" approach is over and we must move on. When the day of emergency arrives, the day of preparation has past.

In a general conference talk, Elder Joseph B. Wirthlin recently told of wolf packs that roamed the countryside of the Ukraine. The defense of the people against these animals was to build large bonfires. He then made the following point relative to testimonies:

> We do not have to protect ourselves from wolf packs as we travel the road of life today, but, in a spiritual sense, we do face the devious wolves of Satan in the form of temptation, evil, and sin. We live in dangerous times when these ravenous wolves roam the spiritual countryside in search of those who may be weak in faith or feeble in their conviction. In his first epistle, Peter described our "adversary the devil, as a roaring lion, [that] walketh about, seeking whom he may devour." (1 Pet. 5:8.) The Lord told the Prophet Joseph Smith that "enemies prowl around thee like wolves for the blood of the lamb." (D&C 122:6.) We are all vulnerable to attack. However, we can fortify ourselves with the protection provided by a burning testimony that, like a bonfire, has been built adequately and maintained carefully.
>
> Unfortunately, some in the Church may believe sin-

cerely that their testimony is a raging bonfire when it really is little more than the faint flickering of a candle. Their faithfulness has more to do with habit than holiness, and their pursuit of personal righteousness almost always takes a back seat to their pursuit of personal interests and pleasure. With such a feeble light of testimony for protection, these travelers on life's highways are easy prey for the wolves of the adversary. . . .

We live in perilous times. The influence of Satan often appears to be unchecked and overwhelming. Remember the promise that God has given to those who build and maintain brightly burning bonfires of testimony to counter the wolves that threaten us. This is His promise: "Fear thou not; for I am with thee: be not dismayed; for I am thy God: I will strengthen thee; yea, I will . . . uphold thee with the right hand of my righteousness." (Isa. 41:10.) (*Ensign,* November 1992, pp. 34, 36.)

This layer of testimony, which will be required in order to stand during the storms ahead, is not received without great effort. Most of our testimonies are on the surface and entirely inadequate to stand the extreme tests at our doorstep. We may never be called upon to die for the kingdom as many early members did, but we must all be willing to do so. Our faith must be that strong. There is a dire need in the Church for a spiritual revival. This life is serious business. We are involved in a literal war, the outcome of which has eternal consequences. To help us with the necessary armor, it is imperative that we strengthen our testimony beyond the surface. Our testimony must be more than skin deep. Joseph Smith said, "The things of God are of deep import; and time, and experience, and careful and ponderous and solemn thoughts can only find them out." (*Teachings of the Prophet Joseph Smith,* p. 137.)

In a training session for General Authorities, President Howard W. Hunter counseled us on this subject. (Keep in mind that he was giving this counsel to General Authorities. We all need to dig even deeper.) He said: "As we are well aware, the world is filled with unknowns; which are rapidly changing and very unpredictable. This is a time when, perhaps more than any other, we need the guidance of the spirit in our deliberations. . . . We need the very special kind of training that can come only by the spirit — that which cannot be taught by any man — that which will be imperative to our success in this work. . . . We need to pay the price to have access to the spiritual promptings and vision that will give our work a proper direction. That price includes an investment of time; it takes quiet time, which generally includes scriptural study, prayer, meditation, and pondering. In other words, ofttimes our work needs to be brooded over. It needs a spiritual context. It needs a spiritual perspective."

I would like to elaborate on the point of paying the price, putting in effort, setting aside some quiet time, and pondering on the things of the Lord. It is easy to get so caught up in the thick of thin things that we don't have time or don't take time for the things that are important. We know that it is a gift, and it is our privilege, to have the whisperings of the Spirit and they usually come when we are relaxed and responsive. Understanding the deeper doctrines and mysteries of the kingdom requires deeper meditation. Gaining a deeper testimony requires deeper commitment. It requires heavy pondering. I like that word *ponder* in describing this search for better understanding and spiritual witness.

Nephi said, "My soul delighteth in the scriptures, and my heart pondereth them." (2 Nephi 4:15.)

Just prior to receiving the vision of the tree of life Nephi said, "As I sat pondering in mine heart I was caught away in the Spirit of the Lord." (1 Nephi 11:1.)

Another Nephi, a few years prior to the birth of the Savior, had a similar experience: "And it came to pass as he was thus pondering in his heart, behold, a voice came unto him saying: Blessed art thou, Nephi." (Helaman 10:3–4.)

Probably the most quoted scripture in the Book of Mormon is Moroni 10:4, wherein Moroni promises us that we can gain a testimony by praying and asking for one. Sometimes overlooked is verse 3: "I would exhort you that when ye shall read these things, . . . ponder it in your hearts."

And finally, in modern times, we read in Doctrine and Covenants 88:62–63: "And again, verily I say unto you, my friends, I leave these sayings with you to ponder in your hearts, . . . that ye shall call upon me while I am near — . . . seek me diligently and ye shall find me; ask, and ye shall receive; knock, and it shall be opened unto you."

What does "to ponder in your hearts" mean? It certainly means more than to fall asleep reading the scriptures each night. It means more than reasoning things out in our minds and intellectualizing over them. To me it means that we long for the truth. We submit ourselves to the truth. We hunger to have the Spirit of the Holy Ghost with us. We literally cry unto the Lord for forgiveness of our sins and plead to be encircled in the arms of his redeeming love. (See Alma 5:9.)

This deeper conviction that goes beyond knowing the

Church is true is crucial in our lives today, let alone for those things which lie ahead. To get into this level of spirituality, we must pay a price that requires walking alone through some adversity.

It has been my experience that the greatest insights are preceded by the darkest hours. They often come at the end of an extreme test of faith. They come when we have been in deep despair but have been faithful in spite of the buffetings of Satan. They come in many different ways, but they do come if we pay the price. They do not come easily. In fact, a profound testimony and personal revelation come as the fruits of obedience, sacrifice, and adversity.

12

Receiving
Personal Revelation

If we are truly obedient, if we learn to sacrifice, and if we endure adversity, we can qualify for increased personal revelation and obtain a deeper testimony. We must increase our capacity to receive personal revelation in these troubled times. I plead for a revival and rededication in each of our lives to pay the price to be worthy to receive and recognize personal revelation.

Those who are honest in heart, if they are willing to study, pray, and put living the commandments to the test, have relatively little trouble receiving a witness that Jesus is the Christ and that Joseph Smith is a prophet of God and was the vehicle through whom the Lord restored the gospel in this dispensation. They may also receive a witness that succeeding prophets received and continue to receive revelation from the Lord. However, it is much harder for us to have confidence in our own ability to receive revelation. A partial explanation of this phenomenon is that we are so well aware of our own imperfections.

Once we have received a witness of the Spirit that the Church is true, we need to move on to learning how we can let that same Spirit become a personal guide. It is extremely important that we gain the confidence and faith that we are individually and personally guided in our lives by that same Spirit which testifies to the divinity of Jesus Christ and the truthfulness of the Church.

Retaining a testimony is a little harder, because once we have received a witness, we must do something about it. Many individuals who receive a testimony become lost along the way because they wander into forbidden paths. Others fail to continue progressing spiritually because they cling to their own abilities and will not make a leap of faith. Still others fail to use their own innate abilities and wait to be miraculously carried to a greater vista without exerting any effort of their own. Either of the latter groups can become disenchanted and frustrated. As a result, they can drift into sitting on the sidelines and criticizing those who are using their best spiritual and physical attributes to move the kingdom forward.

How tragic it will be if we don't each come to grips with our own personal potential and learn the role the Lord has in mind for us. How sad if we waste one more day with a lack of commitment and fail to meet the measure of our creation. When we genuinely lay everything on the altar, an illumination follows that helps us understand what our role is to be in building God's kingdom today. When we accept the gospel as being a reality and lay our all on the altar, we are ready to move on to greater heights.

Unfortunately, most of us are not living up to our potential and are denying ourselves not only additional knowledge of the kingdom, but also a clearer guide in our personal lives. Brigham Young said: "It was asked me by a gentleman how I guided the people by revelation. I teach them to live so that the Spirit of revelation may make plain to them their duty day by day that they are able to guide themselves. To get this revelation it is necessary that the people live so that their spirits are as pure and clean as a piece of blank paper that lies on the desk before the inditer, ready to receive any mark the writer may make upon it." (*Discourses of Brigham Young,* p. 41.)

President Young also explained that "if a person lives according to the revelations given to God's people, he may have the Spirit of the Lord to signify to him his [God's] will, and to guide and to direct him in the discharge of his duties, in his temporal as well as his spiritual exercises. I am satisfied, however, that in this respect, we live far beneath our privileges. . . .

"Thrust a man into prison and bind him with chains, and then let him be filled with the comfort and with the glory of eternity, and that prison is a palace to him. Again, let a man be seated upon a throne with power and dominion in this world, ruling his millions and millions and without that peace which flows from the Lord of Hosts — without that contentment and joy that come from heaven, his palace is a prison; his life is a burden to him; he lives in fear, in dread, and in sorrow. But when a person is filled with the peace and power of God, all is right with him." (Ibid., pp. 32, 33.)

The times in which we live are threatening. We are facing uncertainty on many fronts. In a recent general con-

ference address, Elder Neal A. Maxwell said: "Jesus counseled His disciples, 'Wherefore, settle this in your hearts,
that ye will do the things which I shall teach and command
you.' . . . Being settled keeps us from responding to every
little ripple of dissent as if it were a tidal wave. We are to
be disciples, not oscillators, like a 'reed shaken in the wind.'
(Matt. 11:7.) More members need the immense relief and
peace which can come from being 'settled' without which
those individuals will be like 'the troubled sea, when it
cannot rest.' (Isa. 57:20.)

"There is another special reason to become settled: we
will live in a time in which 'all things shall be in commotion.' (D&C 88:91; 45:26.) The uncertainties, upheavals,
and topsy-turviness of today's world will be such that those
who vacillate and equivocate will be tossed about by severe
turbulence." (*Ensign*, November 1992, p. 67.)

The Prophet Joseph Smith explained that knowledge
"does away with darkness, suspense and doubt." (*Teachings of the Prophet Joseph Smith*, p. 288.) The knowledge
spoken of here refers to personal revelation of the truthfulness of the word of God. Many quote from the Bible
without really believing it. They may think no more of
scriptural quotations than they think of Shakespearian quotations. In order to have current peace and complete hope
and peace in the future, we must have received our knowledge of eternal truth through the manifestation of a spiritual witness. This is a long way of saying we must have
a testimony of the standard works and current prophets.

We are each entitled to receive personal revelation for
living our own lives. The scriptures and current prophets
give us an overview, or architect's plan, but we are individually responsible to build our own eternal lives.

Elder Bruce R. McConkie wrote: "With reference to their own personal affairs, the saints are expected (because they have the gift of the Holy Ghost) to gain personal revelation and guidance rather than to run to the First Presidency or some other church leaders to be told what to do. 'It is a great thing to inquire at the hands of God, or to come into his presence,' the Prophet said, 'and we feel fearful to approach him on subjects that are of little or no consequence, to satisfy the queries of individuals, especially about things the knowledge of which men ought to obtain in all sincerity, before God, for themselves, in humility by the prayer of faith.' (*Teachings*, p. 22.)" (*Mormon Doctrine*, p. 645.)

The scriptures are full of invitations to come to the Lord for personal guidance and answers to our questions and problems. Among them are the following:

"Then shalt thou call, and the Lord shall answer; thou shalt cry, and he shall say, Here I am. . . . And the Lord shall guide thee continually, and satisfy thy soul in drought, and make fat thy bones: and thou shalt be like a watered garden, and like a spring of water, whose waters fail not." (Isaiah 58:9, 11.)

"Be thou humble; and the Lord thy God shall lead thee by the hand, and give thee answer to thy prayers." (D&C 112:10.)

"If ye shall ask with a sincere heart, with real intent, having faith in Christ, he will manifest the truth of it unto you, by the power of the Holy Ghost. And by the power of the Holy Ghost ye may know the truth of all things." (Moroni 10:4–5.)

Sometimes we think of Moroni's promise as pertaining solely to giving us a testimony of the Book of Mormon.

The same power that gives us a testimony of the Book of Mormon can witness the truth of all things.

We often speak of receiving revelation as a defense against the negative influences with which we are faced. Of equal or greater importance is the need to be in tune to take the offense. We are here during this time of this dispensation not to cower in a corner with shields of armor, but to go forward and build the kingdom. This is why I don't really like to whisper of survival; I prefer to shout of revival. Each one of us has a role in building the kingdom. We need to get on with it. We all need to receive a spiritual witness of our own potential.

We need to receive a witness about our specific callings in the Church as well as our roles as family members, missionaries, neighbors, or whatever. There is not one of us who is insignificant in the overall plan. Some of our positions are more visible, but none is more important than any other. We need to know by spiritual witness that we are on the right track to fulfill our eternal destiny. It is one thing to have the bishop tell us the Lord wants us to teach the Blazer Bs. It is quite another to have a personal spiritual witness from the same source.

To illustrate this principle, I would like to share something very personal relative to my call to the Presiding Bishopric. There is some humor here, but the point I will make is very serious.

Just one week prior to April conference 1985, I returned with Elder M. Russell Ballard from Ethiopia, where we had been witnessing the famine firsthand and making certain the offerings the Saints had donated to the Church during the special fast the previous January actually got to the people. At that time, I was the managing director of the

Welfare Services Department of the Church and Elder Ballard was one of the Presidency of the Seventy. As a result of that trip, neither of us will ever be the same. Little did we know our positions in the Church would also be changing. My call to the Presiding Bishopric came one week after I arrived home, and his call to the Quorum of the Twelve came a few months later.

On Friday morning, April 5, 1985, I went to the Assembly Hall on Temple Square to attend a seminar for regional representatives and mission presidents. I held neither of those positions but, because I was the managing director of welfare, I was invited to attend. I sat in the balcony directly above and to the side of the pulpit.

As Elder Thomas S. Monson walked up to take his place on the stand, he caught my eye and gave me a wink. I didn't know what else to do, so I winked back. Then Elder James E. Faust spotted me and, with that contagious smile, he shook his finger at me. I thought to myself, *These brethren are extra friendly this morning. I wonder what I've done.* It was later that I learned my name had been approved the previous day for service in the Presiding Bishopric, and they thought I had already been called. I, of course, at the time didn't have a clue.

When I got back to my office, my secretary informed me that President Gordon B. Hinckley was trying to reach me. Since I had worked quite closely with him on the Ethiopian relief, I assumed it was about some facts and figures that he wanted to use in one of his talks. However, when I entered his office and sat down, he slid his chair back, looked me in the eyes, and said, "Brother Pace, tell me something about yourself."

Then I got nervous. I knew that he had been working

on several major addresses for conference, since both President Kimball and President Romney were ill at that time, but it now occurred to me that he hadn't, in the middle of preparing a talk, suddenly said to himself, "I know what I'd like to do now. I'd like to get better acquainted with that Glenn Pace." No, I knew something was up, and I was soon told that Robert D. Hales was being called to be the Presiding Bishop and that he had recommended that I be called as his second counselor.

I had two shock waves hit me. The first was that I was being called to serve as a General Authority, and the second was that Bishop Hales had recommended me. The reason for the second shock was that he didn't know me. I probably had not spent more than an hour alone with him in my life. Why would he recommend me?

After some more conversation and counsel, President Hinckley asked if I had any questions. I blurted out, "Yes, what do I do? How do I get into the Tabernacle?" I had fears of standing outside rapping on the windows as I was being sustained, unable to get in. I was told I would be given some passes.

I wandered around in a daze for a couple of hours and then went home to tell my wife. We rode around in the car a while and had a good talk, and she shared some of her spiritual feelings. She had been better prepared for the news than I had. As is usually the case, her spiritual sensitivities on this and many other matters were much more finely tuned than mine.

We went into the Tabernacle the next morning with our two passes and handed them to the usher. He wasn't very impressed and pointed toward the back on the north side of the building. I tried to sit on the end so I could get out more easily, but was commanded to slide into the middle of the row and ended up behind a pole. I couldn't understand, because I saw Bishop Henry B. Eyring sitting up front in the middle section, but assumed he was a regional representative.

The next panic I felt was that I could see five empty chairs on the stand, and I knew that three Seventies were going to be called in addition to the change in the Presiding Bishopric. I was certain no one else was sitting as far back as I was, so I pictured myself wandering around up front hunting for a chair long after the next speaker had begun. Thankfully, it dawned on me that the reason for only five chairs was that Bishop Hales was already on the stand because he was currently serving as a member of the Quorum of the Seventy.

The last confidence builder came as I was sustained. It's amazing what can go through your mind in a split second. As President Hinckley announced "Robert D. Hales," a ripple of approval went through the crowd. "Henry B. Eyring" — another ripple. When "Glenn L. Pace" was announced, in my mind's eye I saw a whole sea of shoulders shrug in unison.

I have taken a lot of space here to set up what I am now going to say. It has not been my purpose to make light of sacred things, but to let you understand my anxiety and turmoil during the twenty-four hours following my call. Eighteen hours before my call, I was having a conversation with the Primary president of our ward about the possibility of teaching my seven-year-old daughter's class. Now I found myself sustained as a General Authority.

As soon as that session of conference was over, I made

my way to Bishop Hales. I had not seen or talked to him since my call. He embraced me, and then I asked the deep question of my soul. "I don't understand," I said. "You don't even know me." He answered with words that penetrated my innermost being: "No, I don't know you, but the Lord knows you." He then went on to explain that his recommendation had been discussed in the temple by the First Presidency and Quorum of the Twelve, and they had confirmed his feelings.

This brought great comfort. However, within a few hours I was back in turmoil again. It was wonderful that Bishop Hales knew that the Lord approved of my call. It was a real confidence builder that the Spirit had witnessed the same confirmation to the prophets, seers, and revelators of the kingdom. "Perhaps that should be enough," I told myself. But then the realization hit me. "No, I've got to know for myself."

Consequently, I set about doing those things that would prepare me to receive my own spiritual witness. I knew that the same spirit which manifests the truth of the Book of Mormon is the power by which we "may know the truth of all things" (Moroni 10:4–5) and could give me the personal witness I needed.

With this faith and knowledge, I paid the price and received my personal witness. I knew the answer to my question. It was not given to me to know "Why me?" Rather, it was just "Yes, you."

I want to make another point to all who read these words and may think that my experience was unique to or reserved for only those called to be General Authorities. I want you to know I went through the same process to receive a confirmation about my call to serve as an elders quorum president, a counselor in my ward bishopric, and in many other callings. We don't merely have an *opportunity* to receive a witness relative to our Church calls; we have an *obligation* to do so. The intensity and the vehicle of the witness I received relative to my call as a General Authority was the same as I had received relative to less visible callings. The privilege of receiving such revelation has nothing to do with position, but with worthiness and effort.

Since my call, I have had to renew that witness from time to time. At first I felt guilty going back and asking for more reassurance. However, one day I was reading Joseph Smith's history and discovered that he had to do the same thing. Here was a prophet of God who had seen the Father and the Son. However, he said:

> During the space of time which intervened between the time I had the vision and the year eighteen hundred and twenty-three — having been forbidden to join any of the religious sects of the day, and being of very tender years, and persecuted by those who ought to have been my friends and to have treated me kindly, and if they supposed me to be deluded to have endeavored in a proper and affectionate manner to have reclaimed me — I was left to all kinds of temptations; and, mingling with all kinds of society, I frequently fell into many foolish errors, and displayed the weakness of youth, and the foibles of human nature; which, I am sorry to say, led me into divers temptations, offensive in the sight of God. In making this confession, no one need suppose me guilty of any great or malignant sins. A disposition to commit such was never in my nature. But I was guilty of levity, and sometimes associated with jovial company, etc., not consistent with that character which ought to be maintained by one who was called of God as I had been. But this will not seem very strange to any one

who recollects my youth, and is acquainted with my native cheery temperament.

In consequence of these things, I often felt condemned for my weakness and imperfections; when, on the evening of the above-mentioned twenty-first of September, after I had retired to my bed for the night, I betook myself to prayer and supplication to Almighty God for forgiveness of all my sins and follies, and also for a manifestation to me, that I might know of my state and standing before him; for I had full confidence in obtaining a divine manifestation, as I previously had one. (Joseph Smith–History 1:28–29.)

Of course, we know the rest of the story. All of us, while performing the duties we are assigned, realize we could do better, and we need to know from time to time that we are still right in the sight of God. This is not only our right but also our obligation. Without this confirmation, we will not have the faith required to be successful. All of us have responsibilities in the kingdom beyond our talents. Each calling is larger than the person filling it. The Lord makes up the difference as we, with faith and confidence, do the best we can do. We cannot have that faith unless we know our calling has his approval.

At this writing I am going through the same process to obtain a spiritual witness relative to a new call to the First Quorum of the Seventy. In this case, I was blessed with an impression of the Spirit several months before the call came. On such occasions, we fight such impressions because we wonder if we might be guilty of aspiring to a position. As a general rule, I prefer confirmation to follow a call and not precede it.

As I was released from the Presiding Bishopric, I felt a loss. I didn't know what my assignment would be. Approximately one month after my call to the Seventy, the First Presidency issued an additional call for me to preside over the Sydney Australia North Mission. As soon as the call was issued, I received a witness through the Spirit that it was right. My wife received the same witness.

While the examples I have used have dealt with formal Church callings, the same principle is at play in the full spectrum of life's experiences.

As we function in our formal callings and our less formal — but even more important — roles as parents, children, grandparents, brothers, sisters, and friends, we have access to that same spiritual guidance. There is no limit to our ability to receive revelation.

Elder McConkie said, "Personal revelation is not limited to gaining a testimony and knowing thereby that Jesus, through whom the gospel came, is Lord of all, nor is it limited to receiving guidance in our personal and family affairs — although these are the most common examples of revelation among the Lord's people. In truth and in verity, there is no limit to the revelations each member of the Church may receive. It is within the power of every person who has received the gift of the Holy Ghost to see visions, entertain angels, learn the deep and hidden mysteries of the kingdom." (*A New Witness for the Articles of Faith* [Salt Lake City: Deseret Book, 1985], pp. 489–90.)

With access to divine, personalized revelation, we can each work our way through the trials of these last days, save ourselves unnecessary suffering, and become a moving force in building the kingdom. Many of us think that revelation of the type mentioned by Elder McConkie is reserved for the big issues facing the general Church leaders. I can testify that these experiences are abundant in directing our own lives and in counseling with our children and other individuals needing help.

With all we know about the Lord and his plan, it would be completely out of harmony to think he would guide the Church and not guide the individual members, because the Church *is* its members. I can't overemphasize how strongly I feel that each of us must receive personal revelation during these perilous and beautiful last days.

A caution is in order to conclude this chapter. The ability to recognize when inspiration is being received is difficult to master. The evil one also has ways of communicating. Lucifer sends counterfeit messages and messengers. As Elder McConkie wrote,

> Two spirits are abroad in the earth—one is of God, the other of the devil. The spirit which is of God is one that leads to light, truth, freedom, progress, and every good thing; on the other hand, the spirit which is of Lucifer leads to darkness, error, bondage, retrogression, and every evil thing. One spirit is from above, the other from beneath; and that which is from beneath never allows more light or truth or freedom to exist than it can help. All religion, philosophy, education, science, governmental control—indeed, all things—are influenced and governed by one or the other (in some cases, part by one and part by the other) of these spirits. (Moro. 7.)
>
> It should be understood that these two influences in the world are manifest through the ministrations of actual spirit personages from the unseen world. The power and influence wielded by Satan is exercised through the host of evil spirits who do his bidding and who have power, according to laws that exist, to impress their wills upon the minds of receptive mortals. On the other hand, much of the power and influence of Deity is exercised by and manifest through spirit beings who

appear and give revelation and guidance as the Lord's purposes may require. In general, the more righteous and saintly a person is, the easier it will be for him to receive communications from heavenly sources; and the more evil and corrupt he is, the easier will it be for evil spirits to implant their nefarious schemes in his mind and heart. (*Mormon Doctrine,* pp. 270–71.)

It is my observation that those who get into trouble on this issue are those who are more anxious to receive personal revelation from God than they are to keep the commandments God has already revealed to his prophets. Their reasons for wanting personal revelation are not pure. They covet the perceived power of this communication more than they desire purity. They want to be able to speak for him without being willing to become like him. Satan hears their petitions, obliges their requests, and leads them carefully and deceptively into darker practices. Such individuals often lead more innocent, but naive, people astray with them by disclosing their "revelation" to anyone and everyone who will listen.

Others lead themselves away by their own "intellectual bungee jumping," as Elder Maxwell has put it. These are they who, in my train analogy, keep trying to run ahead of the train. They feel that the train is going too slowly or that their wisdom and foresight are ahead of the prophets'. They too lead others who in their naivete are captivated by silver tongues and intellectual mumbo jumbo.

President Spencer W. Kimball gave us the key to prevent being coaxed off of the train:

Following leaders is the path of safety. Every normal person may have a sure way of knowing what is right and what is wrong. He may learn the gospel and receive the Holy Spirit which will always guide him as to right and wrong. In addition to this, he has the leaders of the Lord's church. And the only sure, safe way is to follow that leadership—follow the Holy Spirit within you and follow the prophets, dead and living.

No one in this Church will ever go far astray who ties himself securely to the authorities whom the Lord has placed in his Church. This Church will never go astray; the Quorum of the Twelve will never lead you into bypaths; it never has and never will. There could be individuals who would falter; there will never be a majority of the Council of the Twelve on the wrong side at any time. The Lord has chosen them; he has given them specific responsibilities. And those people who stand close to them will be safe. And, conversely, whenever one begins to go his own way in opposition to authority, he is in grave danger. I would not say that those leaders whom the Lord chooses are necessarily the most brilliant, nor the most highly trained, but they are the chosen, and when chosen of the Lord they are his recognized authority, and the people who stay close to them have safety. (*Teachings of Spencer W. Kimball,* p. 459.)

Elder Boyd K. Packer recently issued a warning and some counsel on this subject to those who want to run ahead of the train and to those who are tempted to jump off and follow them. After quoting from Doctrine and Covenants 42:11, where the Lord said, "It shall not be given to any one to go forth to preach my gospel, or to build up my church, except he be ordained by some one who has authority, and it is known to the church that he has authority and has been regularly ordained by the heads of the church," he commented:

There are some among us now who have *not* been

regularly ordained by the heads of the Church who tell of impending political and economic chaos, the end of the world—something of the "sky is falling, chicken licken" of the fables. They are misleading members to gather to colonies or cults.

Those deceivers say that the Brethren do not know what is going on in the world or that the Brethren approve of their teaching but do not wish to speak of it over the pulpit. Neither is true. The Brethren, by virtue of traveling constantly everywhere on earth, certainly know what is going on, and by virtue of prophetic insight are able to read the signs of the times.

Do not be deceived by them—those deceivers. If there is to be any gathering, it will be announced by those who have been regularly ordained and who are known to the Church to have authority.

Come away from any others. Follow your leaders who have been duly ordained and have been publicly sustained, and you will not be led astray. (*Ensign*, November 1992, p. 73.)

We should always measure the content of our own personal inspiration against what has been revealed through the prophets. We should also become very leery of anything we receive which is out of our area of jurisdiction. On this, President Kimball said:

Individual revelations will harmonize with Church program. The one who receives revelation for any part of the Church, if his revelations are from God, will always be in the same direction as the general program the Lord has revealed to his prophets. In other words, the Lord will never reveal to a bishop a new program entirely contradictory to the program of the Church, even for his own ward. His revelations to the bishop, to the stake president, the mission president, will be more or less confirming and amplifying and giving further details. So each individual is entitled to the revelations of the Lord, call it inspiration if you want to, it's a matter of degree largely.

Revelations come in one's area of responsibility. The father and mother of the family are entitled to revelation for the ruling of their family and all of their interests. The bishop is entitled to the revelations of God for his flock; the stake president for the stake, and the President of the Church, of course, is the only one that holds the keys actively and totally, and he will receive the revelations for the Church.

Whenever an individual gets out of his area and begins to tell the bishop of revelations he's received for the conduct of the ward, then he's wrong. His revelations are coming from the wrong source because God is not the author of confusion. (*Teachings of Spencer W. Kimball*, p. 453.)

With these cautions, I once again beseech the members of the Church to qualify themselves to receive the personal revelation to which they are entitled, and to recognize the fact that the prophets, seers, and revelators are receiving the revelations to which they are entitled for the general direction of the Church.

This is a wonderful time to be living. The challenges and joys for those who are actively building the kingdom couldn't be more fulfilling and will lead to eternal joy. Personally, when my time comes to pass through the veil and I am able to meet Joseph, Brigham, people who died crossing the plains, and my own great-great-grandparents, I want to be free of regrets. I want to share with them how I met the assignments given to me, and to listen to the details of their experiences. I want to live worthy of the heritage I've been given. This is truly our hour of opportunity.

I pray that the thoughts in this book have increased your yearnings for these and many other righteous desires. Let's all get on the train and stay on until we reach our final destination of eternal life together with our Father in heaven, the Lord Jesus Christ, and our relatives and friends.

Index

Abrea, Angel, 133–34
Adversity. *See* Calamities;
Natural disasters; Trials
Africa: stories of Saints in, 49–63;
leadership conference in, 153–56
Alma the Younger, 140–42, 144
"Armageddon mentality," 7
Armor of God, 74–75

Ballard, M. Russell, 13–14, 71–72, 84–85, 159–60, 178–79
Baptism of earth, 16–17
Benson, Ezra Taft, 52, 67, 133, 154–55
Bishops, role of, in caring for poor, 82–83
Bonfire, testimony likened to, 168–69
Brethren, following, 66, 187–89
Brown, Victor L., 111

Calamities: increase in, 17–18;
working to prevent, 23–24;
taking satisfaction in, 25–26;
succoring victims of, 26–30;
safety in, 70–74
Callings, receiving personal revelation regarding, 178–85
Cannon, George Q.: on spiritual destruction, 14; on natural disasters, 15; on people's blindness to fulfilled prophecies, 17; on rationalizations about calamities, 18; on war, 71; on sacrifice, 152
Celestial kingdom: law of, 8;
three degrees in, 109;
importance of marriage in, 124–25
Child: hurt, analogy of, 21–22;
becoming as, 62–63
Church of Jesus Christ of Latter-day Saints: likened to train, 2–